ZF GEARS (Great Britain) LTD.

Kernel One

Robert O'Neill

STUDENTS' BOOK

With contributions from **Alan McLean** to the Read and Write sections

Longman

LONGMAN GROUP LIMITED
London

*Associated companies, branches and representatives
throughout the world*

© Longman Group Ltd 1978

First published 1978
New impression 1979

ISBN 0 582 51925 X

Illustrated by John Walsh

We are grateful to Barnaby's Picture Library for
permission to reproduce the photographs on page 2.

ACKNOWLEDGEMENTS

Two people have collaborated directly on certain aspects
of the material: Alan McLean (Read and Write sections)
and David Mills (Review, Word List, List of Verbs etc.).
They also gave me valuable advice and criticism while the
material was being written.

There were many other people who helped me in the
various phases of the conception and execution of this
book. I should like to mention in particular Waldo
Bindseil, Gareth Thomas, Rosalyn Hurst and Erhard
Waespi of Eurocentres.

Robert O'Neill, 1978

The publishers should like to thank Mr Erh. J. C. Waespi
and Mr R. Schärer of the Foundation for European
Language and Educational Centres, Zurich, whose
encouragement and suggestions were of great help in the
preparation of the material.

Our thanks are also given to the principal and staff of
Eurocentre Bournemouth, for their very useful suggestions and advice.

The Eurocentres are a group of language schools directed
by the Foundation for European Language and
Educational Centres, Zurich. The schools offer full-time
courses for adult students all the year round, and each
language is taught in the country where it is spoken.

Printed in Great Britain by
Spottiswoode Ballantyne Ltd. Colchester and London

Contents

Unit 1 **Hello**
What's your name?
Where are you from?
What's the time?

Unit 2 **On the plane**
I'm going to London.
Is this/that your suitcase?
Where are you going?

Unit 3 **On the train**
What time is the train?
Which platform?
How much is the ticket?

Unit 4 **In London**
We're over London now.
I can see Big Ben.
Can you see it, too?

Unit 5 **The airport**
What have you got in your
suitcase? – Only clothes.
Hmm! What's this? Four
bottles of whisky!

Unit 6 **A room for the night**
Is there a lift in the hotel?
Janet can see Hyde Park from
her window. What can Terry
see?

Unit 7 **A job in Camden Town**
Can you type?
How many words a minute?
Can you speak French?

Unit 8 **Monday morning**
Laura lives in Watford.
She works in London.
Where do you live?

Unit 9 **Watching Janet**
She always gets up at 7.
She usually leaves at 9.
When do you get up?

Unit 10 **The burglar**
There's a man in Mike's flat.
I don't know him. He doesn't
live there.

Unit 11 **Friday evening**
Do you like pizza?
I don't want any wine.
Do you want some coffee?

Unit 12 **Saturday morning**
What do you want to do this
evening? Let's go to the
cinema.

Unit 13 **Frank's last day in prison**
He was in prison yesterday.
Where were you yesterday?

Unit 14 **Laura's old job**
Laura worked in an office last
year. Where did you work?

Unit 15 **A job for Frank?**
He got up at 7 yesterday.
He went to an interview.
What did you do yesterday?

Unit 16 **The kidnapping**
Terry didn't see Janet
yesterday. Why didn't she
come to the cinema?

Unit 17 **The telephone call**
Is Janet going to see her father
again? What are they going to
do?

Unit 18 **A million dollars!**
Mr Snow has to find a million
dollars. What does he have to
do then?

Goodbye
What happened in the factory?
Did Janet get away?
What about Lucky?

pages 107–116
READ AND WRITE 1 (for use after Unit 6)
READ AND WRITE 2 (for use after Unit 9)
READ AND WRITE 3 (for use after Unit 12)
READ AND WRITE 4 (for use after Unit 15)
READ AND WRITE 5 (for use after Unit 18)
Review (page 117)
Days, Months, Numbers (page 125)
List of Verbs with Past Tense forms (page 125)
Word List (page 127)

Unit 1 Hello

MIKE: Hello. My name is Mike Sutton.

ANNA: And my name is Anna Parker. Hello.

MIKE: What's your name?
ANNA: Anna Parker. What's your name?
MIKE: Mike Sutton.
ANNA: Hello.
MIKE: Hello.

MIKE: Anna.
ANNA: Yes?
MIKE: What's the time?
ANNA: It's one o'clock. Look!
MIKE: Thank you.

1 2 3
4 5 6

One	Two	Three
Four	Five	Six

b

1

What's the time?   It's ___ o'clock.

2

PICTURE ONE
This is London.
London is a city.
It is in England.

PICTURE TWO
And this is New York.
New York is a city, too.
It isn't in England.
It is in America.

PICTURE THREE
This is Big Ben.
Big Ben is a clock and
it is in London.

PICTURE FOUR
And this is Broadway.
Broadway is a street in
New York.

3 ASK and ANSWER

Is ___ in ___ ? → **Yes, it is.**
                  No, it isn't.

Is London in America?   No, it isn't.

1. ___ London in England?   Yes, it ___
2. ___ New York in England?   No, it ___
3. ___ New York in America?   ___, it ___

4. ___ Big Ben in New York?   ___, ___ ___
5. ___ Big Ben ___ London?   ___, ___ ___
6. ___ Broadway ___ London?   ___, ___ ___
7. ___ Broadway ___ New York?   ___, ___ ___

2

1

 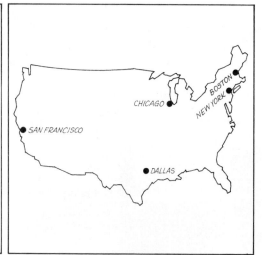

England is a country and America is a country, too.

Bristol is a city in England. Liverpool is in England, too.

Dallas is in America. San Francisco is a city in America, too.

Where is Chicago? Where is Manchester? Where is Leeds? And where is Boston?

2

Where is ___? → It is (It's) in ___

3

Liverpool   Bristol

London

Look at Anna and Mike

She is in London. He is in London, too.

Mike isn't from London. He is from Liverpool.

And Anna? She is from Bristol.

4

Is	Mike Anna	in from	America? New York? England? London? Liverpool? Bristol?	→	Yes,	he she	**is**.
					No,	he she	**isn't**.

d

1

Listen, please!

MIKE: Where are you from, Anna?
ANNA: Pardon?
MIKE: Where are you from?
ANNA: Bristol.
MIKE: Oh.
ANNA: And where are you from?
MIKE: I'm from Liverpool.
ANNA: Oh.

2 *Stop and Look*

YOU SAY   YOU WRITE

He				
She	's	I'm		
It		You're		

He		I am
She	is	
It		You are

3

is am are He She It in from

England ___ a country. = *England is a country.*

1. Big Ben ___ a clock in London.
2. Mike Sutton is ___ London.
3. ___ is ___ Liverpool.
4. Anna Parker ___ from Bristol.
5. ___ is in London.
6. London ___ a city.
7. ___ is in England.

4 What about you?

1. Where ___ you from?
2. I ___ from ___
3. My name ___ ___ ___

4

This is Janet Snow.
She is in a street in New York.
A taxi is coming.
It is eight o'clock.

JANET: Taxi! Taxi!

She is in the taxi now.

TAXI DRIVER: Where to?
JANET: Kennedy Airport.

Where is the taxi going?
It is going to Kennedy Airport.
Where is Janet going?
She is going to Kennedy Airport, too.

And this is Kennedy Airport.
Look! A plane is arriving.
The plane is coming from London.

Janet is at Kennedy Airport.

JANET: Good morning. I'm going to London.
STEWARDESS: London? Your ticket, please.
JANET: Here you are.
STEWARDESS: And is this your suitcase?
JANET: No, that's my suitcase.
And that's my suitcase, too.

a *Answer the questions*

| Yes, | he she it | **is**. | No, | he she it | **isn't**. |

PICTURE ONE

1. Is Janet in London?
2. Is she in England?
3. Is she in New York?
4. Is a taxi coming?

PICTURE TWO

1. Is Janet in the taxi?
2. Is the taxi driver in the taxi?

PICTURE THREE

1. Is Janet going to New York?
2. Is she going to Kennedy Airport?
3. Is the taxi going to Kennedy Airport, too?

PICTURE FOUR

1. Is this London Airport?
2. Is it Kennedy Airport?
3. Look at the plane. Is it going to London?
4. Is it coming from London?

PICTURE FIVE

1. Is Janet in the taxi?
2. Is she going to the airport?
3. Is she at the airport?
4. Is she going to London?

b

Stop and Say

1

| **7** | **8** | **9** | **10** | **11** | **12** |
| Seven | Eight | Nine | Ten | Eleven | Twelve |

What's the time?   **It's ___ o'clock.**

2

Open dialogue

STEWARDESS: Is this your ___?
YOU: No, it isn't.
            That's my ___

coat   book   newspaper

bag   camera   briefcase

3

ASK and ANSWER

Is the plane { **going to ___?** / **coming from ___?** }

Where is it { **going?** / **coming from?** }

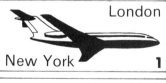
London / New York   **1**

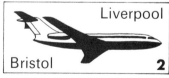
Liverpool / Bristol   **2**

New York / Liverpool   **3**

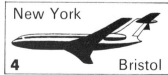
New York / Bristol   **4**

6

1

And now look at this man. His name is George King. George is in New York, too. He is in a hotel. George is from London.
Listen! He is speaking to a clerk.

CLERK: Good morning, Mr King.
GEORGE: Good morning. Call me a taxi, please.
CLERK: A taxi? Yes, sir.

2

It is eight fifteen now.

CLERK: Mr King! Your taxi is here.
GEORGE: Thank you.
CLERK: Is that your suitcase?
GEORGE: Yes, it is. Where's the porter?
CLERK: Porter!
GEORGE: I'm going to the taxi now.
CLERK: Yes, sir. The porter is coming.

3

Listen to the taxi driver and to George.

TAXI DRIVER: Where are you going?
GEORGE: Kennedy Airport.
TAXI DRIVER: Kennedy Airport! Right! Get in.

4

It is nine fifteen now and George is at Kennedy Airport.

GEORGE: I'm going to London. Here's my ticket.
STEWARDESS: Thank you. And where's your suitcase?
GEORGE: Here.
STEWARDESS: Put it on the scale, please. Hmm. Eighteen kilos. That's OK, sir. Thank you.

PICTURE ONE

1. Look at the man. What is his name?
2. Where is he from?
3. Where is he now?
4. Is he speaking to Janet Snow?

PICTURE TWO

1. What is the time?
2. Is the taxi here?
3. Is George in the taxi?
4. Is he going to the taxi?

PICTURE THREE

1. Is George at Kennedy Airport now?
2. Is he in a street in New York?
3. Where is he going?
4. Where is the taxi driver?

PICTURE FOUR

1. Where is George now?
2. What is the time?
3. Is George going to Dallas?
4. Is he going to Liverpool?
5. Where is he going?
6. And where is his suitcase?

d

1

It is eleven fifteen now. Janet Snow and George King are on a plane. The plane isn't arriving. It is going to London.

1. ___ the plane going to New York? No, it ___
2. Where is it ___? It is ___ to London.
3. ___ Janet ___ to London? Yes, ___ is.
4. ___ George ___ to London, too? Yes, ___ ___

2

STEWARDESS: Where ___ ___ going, sir?
GEORGE: I'm ___ to London.
STEWARDESS: ___ is ___ ticket, please?
GEORGE: Here.
STEWARDESS: Thank ___. And ___ that ___ suitcase?
GEORGE: No, ___ ___. This ___ ___ suitcase.

3 **Stop and Say**

13 14 15 16 17 18

Thirteen Fourteen Fifteen Sixteen Seventeen Eighteen

4

A taxi ___ coming. = *A taxi is coming.*

1. George ___ in a taxi.
2. He ___ ___ to Kennedy Airport.
3. Janet is ___ a taxi, too.
4. ___ is ___ to Kennedy Airport, ___
5. And now ___ time ___ eleven fifteen.
6. Janet is on ___ plane.
7. She is going ___ London.
8 George is on the ___, too.
9. ___ is going to ___, too.

Look at this man and this woman.
His name is Terry Carter and her name is Laura Francis.
They are in Liverpool.
Look at the time, too.
It is six thirty.

This is Lime Street Station.
It is a big station in Liverpool.
Look at platform seven. That is the train to London. The train to London is at platform seven.

Laura Francis is at Lime Street Station.
Listen.

LAURA: What time is the train to London, please?
CLERK: Six forty.
LAURA: And which platform, please?
CLERK: Platform seven.
LAURA: Thank you.

Terry Carter is at Lime Street Station, too.
Listen. He is buying a ticket.

TERRY: London, please.
CLERK: Single or return?
TERRY: Single, please.
CLERK: Twelve pounds.
TERRY: Pardon? How much?
CLERK: Twelve pounds.

Liverpool to London SINGLE

Liverpool to London RETURN

a

PICTURE ONE

1. Look at that man.
   What is his name?
2. Look at that woman.
   What is her name?
3. Where is he?
4. Is she in Liverpool, too?

PICTURE TWO

1. Where is Lime Street
   Station?
2. Is it a big station?
3. Where is the train to
   London?

PICTURE THREE

1. Where is Laura now?
2. What time is her train?
3. Where is she going?

PICTURE FOUR

1. What is Terry buying?
2. Where is he going?
3. How much is his ticket?

b

1 (Stop and Say)

19 20 30 40 50 60

Nineteen Twenty Thirty Forty Fifty Sixty

2

What's the time, please?
It's ___ ___

3

You are going to Bristol.
You are buying a return ticket.

YOU: ___, ___
CLERK: Single or return?
YOU: ___. ___ ___?
CLERK: Nine pounds ten.

4

What time is the train to ___?
Which platform?
How much is a ticket to ___?

DESTINATION	PLATFORM	TIME	FARE
London	7	6.40	£12
Leeds	5	7.15	£ 4.40
Bristol	2	7.20	£ 9.10
Manchester	6	7.30	£ 2.50

1 It is six forty now and the train is leaving. It is going to London. Laura and Terry are on the train. He is going to London and she is going to Watford. Watford is near London.

2

ASK and ANSWER

1. What ___ ___ time?
2. Where ___ ___ train going?
3. ___ Terry on ___ train?
4. ___ Laura ___ ___ train, too?
5. Where ___ he going?
6. ___ she ___ to London, too?
7. Where ___ ___ going?
8. Where ___ Watford?

3

This is the buffet car. Terry is buying a coffee. What is Laura buying? *Listen*

WAITER: Yes, sir?
TERRY: A coffee, please.
WAITER: Twenty p, please. Yes, madam?
LAURA: Tea, please.
WAITER: Eighteen p, please.

Terry and Laura are talking. *Listen*

LAURA: Excuse me. Is this seat taken?
TERRY: No, it isn't.
LAURA: Thank you.
TERRY: Cigarette?
LAURA: Oh, thanks!
TERRY: Where are you going?
LAURA: To Watford.
TERRY: Oh. I'm going to London.
LAURA: Oh.

d

MENU

COFFEE	20p	**SANDWICHES**	
TEA	18p	BEEF	40p
COCA-COLA	20p		
BEER	30p	EGG & TOMATO	30p
		CHEESE	30p

SOUP

 TOMATO 30p

CHICKEN 30p

1 This is the menu in the buffet car.

How much is a ___?
A ___ is ___ p.

2

You are buying a coffee and a beef sandwich.

WAITER: Yes, ___?
YOU: A ___ and a ___ ___, please.
WAITER: ___ p, please.
YOU: Pardon? ___ much?
WAITER: ___ ___, ___

And now you are speaking to Terry.

YOU: Excuse ___. Is this seat ___?
TERRY: No, ___ ___
YOU: Where ___ you ___?
TERRY: I'm ___ to London. Where ___ ___ ___?
YOU: ___ ___ to London, too.

3  *Stop and Look*

He She	is	going to ___
I	am	

Where	is	he she	going?
	are	you	

YOU SAY

He She It	's	going
	I'm	
	You're	

YOU WRITE

He She It	is	going
	I am	
	You are	

4  *Write*

Her   His   My
is   am   going
I   He   She

___ name ___ Terry Carter.
___ is ___ to London.

___ name ___ Laura Francis.
___ is ___ to Watford.

TERRY: ___ name ___ Terry Carter.
         ___ ___ going ___ London.

LAURA: ___ name ___ Laura Francis.
         ___ ___ ___ to Watford.

a

This is Big Ben in London. Look at the time.
It is nine o'clock in the evening now.
Can you see that plane up there?
Janet Snow and George King are on it. They are coming from New York.
It is raining in London.

Janet can see Big Ben. She is speaking to a woman.

JANET: We're over London now.
WOMAN: Are we?
JANET: Yes. Look down there! I can see Big Ben.
WOMAN: Oh, yes. I can see it too. Is it raining?
JANET: Yes, it is.

George King is smoking a big cigar.
The stewardess is speaking to him.

STEWARDESS: Excuse me, sir. You're smoking.
GEORGE: What? Pardon?
STEWARDESS: You're smoking, sir. No smoking, please. We're over London. We're arriving now.

What about Terry Carter and Laura Francis?
They are in Watford now. He is on the train.
She is on the platform. It's raining in Watford, too.

TERRY: Well, goodbye, Laura. Here's your suitcase.
LAURA: Thanks, Terry. Goodbye.

a

PICTURE ONE

1. *Speak about the picture.*
   Say
   I can see . . .

2. *Ask questions about the picture*
   ___ ___ ___ time?
   Where ___ ___ ___ ___ ?
   Can you see ___ ___ ?

Answer the questions

PICTURE TWO
1. Where is Janet now?
2. Is George on the plane, too?
3. What can Janet see?
4. Is it raining?

PICTURE THREE

1. Is the stewardess smoking?
2. Is George smoking?
3. What is he smoking?
4. Is the plane arriving now?
5. Where is it arriving?

PICTURE FOUR

Ask and answer
1. Where ___ ___ ?
2. Is ___ on the ___?
3. ___ ___ raining?
4. Terry is saying:
   "Well, goodbye, Laura. Here's
   your suitcase."
   What is Laura saying?

b

1

He   She   They

Janet is on a plane. = *She is on a plane.*
Janet and George are on a plane. = *They are on a plane.*

1 Janet is over London.
2. Janet and George are over London.
3. Terry and Laura are in Watford.
4. Laura is from Watford.
5. Terry is on the train.
6. Laura is on the platform.
7. Mike and Anna are in London.
8. Anna is from Bristol.
9. Mike is from Liverpool.
10. Terry and Mike are from Liverpool.

2   (Stop and Look)

He She It } **is in** ___	I **am in** ___	They We You } **are in** ___

3

You are on the plane and you are speaking to the stewardess.

YOU: Excuse ___. ___ we over London now?
STEWARDESS: Yes, ___ are. And ___ ___ arriving in a minute.
YOU: ___ ___ raining in London?
STEWARDESS: Yes, ___ ___
YOU: And ___ ___ ___ time, please?
STEWARDESS: ___ nine ___
YOU: Thank ___

C

1

You can see two pictures. One picture is on the left. The other picture is on the right.
In one picture you can see London Airport. In the other picture you can see Euston Station. Euston is a big station in London.

You can see a plane and a train, too. They are arriving in London. Which is the plane? Which is the train? And which is London Airport? Which is Euston Station?

2

Where is . . . ?   Is that . . . ?   Is the ___ arriving in ___?

3

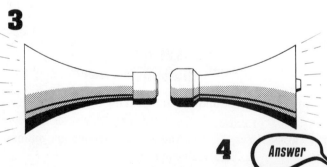

You can hear two loudspeakers, too. *Listen*

LOUDSPEAKER ONE: The train from Liverpool is arriving at platform four.

LOUDSPEAKER TWO: Pan Am announces the arrival of flight four seven nine oh from New York.

4 Answer

1. What can you see in the picture on the left?
2. What can you see on the right?
3. Where is Euston?
4. Is the plane arriving at Euston?
5. Where is it arriving?
6. Is the train arriving at Euston?
7. Which platform is it arriving at?
8. Where is it coming from?
9. And what about the plane? Where is it coming from?

c

5

train ___ arriving ___ London. = *The train is arriving in London.*

1. ___ train is ___ from ___
2. ___ plane ___ arriving ___ New York.
3. Janet ___ on ___ plane.

4. Terry ___ on ___ train.
5. They ___ arriving ___ London now.
6. George King ___ ___ ___ plane, too.

d

1

Terry Carter is phoning Mike Sutton now.
Listen

MIKE: Five nine four, three oh six eight.
TERRY: Hello? Is that Mike? Mike Sutton?
MIKE: Yes. Who's that?
TERRY: It's Terry.
MIKE: Pardon? Who?
TERRY: It's Terry!
MIKE: Terry! Where are you?
TERRY: I'm at Euston Station.
MIKE: Where? Euston Station? Are you in London?
TERRY: Yes, that's right. I'm in London now!

2

And now you are phoning Mike Sutton. You are at London Airport.

MIKE: Hello?
YOU: Hello. Is ___ Mike Sutton?
MIKE: Yes. ___'s that?
YOU: ___'s ___
MIKE: Pardon? Who?
YOU: ___ ___ ___
MIKE: ___! Where ___ you?
YOU: ___ ___ London Airport.
MIKE: Where? London Airport! ___ ___ in England?
YOU: Yes, ___'s right. ___ ___ England now!

3

Who? Where?

Who ___ ___? = *Who is that?*
It is Terry Carter.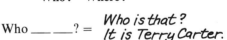

Where ___ ___? = *Where is he?*
He is at Euston Station.

1. ___ ___ that?
   ___ ___ Janet Snow.

2. ___ ___ she?
   ___ ___ at London Airport.

3. ___ ___ ___?
   ___ ___ George King.

4. ___ ___ ___?
   ___ ___ ___ London Airport, too.

1

The passengers on Flight 4790 from New York are at London Airport now. They are waiting. They are waiting for their suitcases. Their suitcases are coming now. Janet and George are waiting, too. George is wearing a coat and hat. What about Janet?

2

George has got his suitcase now. Janet has got her suitcases, too. He has got one suitcase and she has got two suitcases. Janet has got a porter. He is carrying her suitcases.

3

This man is at London Airport. His name is Tracey. A policewoman is looking at him. He isn't looking at her. Tracey hasn't got a suitcase. And he hasn't got a ticket. He has got an umbrella. Can you see it? He is carrying it.

4

This is Anna Parker again. Janet is her friend. Anna is in the car park at London Airport. It is raining and she hasn't got an umbrella. That is her car. It is in the car park, too.

a

Say **That's right.**
　　That's wrong.

Janet is on the plane.
= **That's wrong.**

She is at London Airport.
= **That's right.**

PICTURE ONE

1. The passengers are waiting for a plane.
2. Janet is waiting for her suitcases.
3. They are coming.
4. She is wearing a coat.
5. He is wearing a coat and hat.

PICTURE TWO

1. Janet isn't waiting now.
   She has got her suitcases.
2. George is waiting.
3. He has got his suitcase.
4. A porter is carrying it.

Now answer the questions

PICTURE THREE

1. Who is this man?
2. Where is he?
3. Is he carrying a suitcase?
4. What is he carrying?
5. What is he wearing?

PICTURE FOUR

1. And who is this?
2. Where is she?
3. Has she got a car?
4. Where is it?

b

1

Stop and Look

			a suitcase.
He			an umbrella.
	has	got	a bag.
	hasn't		a ticket.
She			etc.

2

Stop and Say

He**'s got** a newspaper. He **hasn't got** a ticket.
She**'s got** two suitcases. She **hasn't got** a bag.

3

You can see eight things in the picture. George has got four.
And Janet has got four.
In the picture you can see:

1. a box of cigars
2. a pair of jeans
3. a bottle of whisky
4. a bottle of perfume
5. a dress　6. a suit
7. a blouse　8. a shirt

Speak about George and Janet

He's got a ___ in **his** suitcase.
She's got a ___ in **her** suitcase.

1

The policewoman is speaking to Tracey.
Listen

POLICEWOMAN:	Excuse me.
TRACEY:	Yes?
POLICEWOMAN:	Are you waiting for a plane?
TRACEY:	Yes, I am. For the New York plane.
POLICEWOMAN:	Well, have you got a ticket? Have you got a passport?
TRACEY:	No, I haven't. But I'm not going to New York. I'm waiting for the plane from New York. A friend is coming on it.

4

Now listen to Anna and Janet

ANNA:	Janet! I'm over here! Hi!
JANET:	Anna! Hello!
ANNA:	Have you got your suitcases?
JANET:	Yes, I have. A porter is bringing them.
ANNA:	Good! I've got my car here. It's in the car park. Come on. I can take you to your hotel.
JANET:	Oh, good! Thanks! Porter! We're going to the car park. Bring my suitcases, please.
ANNA:	It's raining and I haven't got an umbrella. Have you got one?
JANET:	No, I haven't.

2

Has Tracey **got** a ___ ? → Yes, he **has**.
No, he **hasn't**.

Is he **going** to ___ ___ ?
Is he **waiting** for ___ ___ ? → Yes, he **is**.
No, he **isn't**.

5

Has { Janet, Anna, the porter } **got** ___ ___ ?

Is . . . ?

3

Now speak about Tracey

He **hasn't got** a ___
He **isn't going** to ___ ___
He**'s waiting** for ___ ___
His friend **is coming** on the ___

6

Now speak about the conversation

Anna has got ___ ___ . It . . .
The porter is . . . They are going to . . .
Anna hasn't got ___ ___ . Janet hasn't got ___ ___

d

1

Stop and Look

I We You They	have got/haven't got ___	Have	I we you they	got ___?	→	Yes, ___ have. No, ___ haven't.
He She	has got/hasn't got ___	Has	he she	got ___?	→	Yes, ___ has. No, ___ hasn't.

YOU WRITE

I **have got** a car.
We **have got** four suitcases.
She **has got** two suitcases.
He **has got** an umbrella.

YOU SAY

I**'ve got** a car.
We**'ve got** four suitcases.
She**'s got** two suitcases.
He**'s got** an umbrella.

2

Look at Terry Carter again.
He is walking to a hotel near Euston Station. What
has he got? What hasn't he got?

___ he ___ a car? No, ___ ___
= *Has he got a car? No, he hasn't.*

1. ___ he ___ a bag? Yes, ___ ___
2. ___ he ___ a suitcase? No, ___ ___
3. ___ he ___ a hat? ___, ___ ___
4. ___ he ___ an umbrella? ___, ___ ___

3

What about you?

Have you got these things?
a car = *I have got a car.*
    or *I haven't got a car.*

1. a passport
2. a ticket to New York
3. a friend in New York
4. a friend in London
5. a raincoat   6. an umbrella
7. a dress   8. a suit
9. a shirt   10. a blouse

4

Ask people in your class

Have you **got** a ___? → Yes, I **have**.
No, I **haven't**.

1. a passport
2. a ticket to New York
3. a friend in ___   4. a car
5. . . .   6. . . .

20

1 You can see two hotels in this picture. One of them is near Hyde Park (a big park in London). The other is near Euston Station.

The hotel on the left is called "The Park Hotel". It has got two hundred rooms. It is big. The hotel on the right is called "York House". It has got twenty rooms. It is small.

"York House" is between a pub and a garage.

A room at "The Park Hotel" is £30 a night. A room at "York House" is £5 a night. "The Park Hotel" is expensive and "York House" is cheap.

Which hotel is Janet going to? Is she going to "The Park Hotel" or to "York House"? Which hotel is Terry going to?

2

1. **Has** $\begin{cases} \text{"The Park Hotel"} \\ \text{"York House"} \end{cases}$ **got** ___ rooms?

2. **Is** ___ $\begin{cases} \text{big} \\ \text{small} \end{cases}$?

3. **Is** ___ **going** to ___?

4. **How much** is a room at ___?

5. **Is** ___ $\begin{cases} \text{cheap} \\ \text{expensive} \end{cases}$?

3

You are asking Janet questions.
What are they?

1. YOU: . . . ?
   JANET: Oh, I'm going to a hotel called "The Park Hotel".

2. YOU: . . . ?
   JANET: Yes, it is. It's got two hundred rooms.

3. YOU: . . . ?
   JANET: £30 a night.

4. YOU: . . . ?
   JANET: It's in Park Lane, near Hyde Park.

f

1

George King isn't going to a hotel. A customs officer is asking him questions at the airport. *Listen*

OFFICER: One moment, sir. Wait.
GEORGE: Who? Me?
OFFICER: Yes. You, sir. How many suitcases have you got?
GEORGE: Only one. This one.
OFFICER: And what have you got in it?
GEORGE: Clothes.
OFFICER: Clothes? Only clothes?
GEORGE: Yes, only clothes. I've got two suits, three shirts and a pair of shoes. Oh, and I've got four pairs of socks.
OFFICER: Hmm. Open your suitcase, please.
GEORGE: Open it? But . . . but . . . I . . . I . . .
OFFICER: Hmm. What's this? Four bottles of whisky! And you've got three boxes of cigars, too. Fifty in this box, fifty in this one and fifty in this one, too. You've got one hundred and fifty cigars! So, you've only got clothes, eh? Tell me. Can you wear a cigar, sir? And can you wear a bottle of whisky, too?

2

1. How many suitcases has George got?
2. Has he only got clothes in it?
3. How many bottles of whisky has he got?
4. How many boxes of cigars has he got?
5. How many cigars has he got?
6. What clothes has he got in his suitcase?

3 *Stop and Say*

70	**76**	**80**
Seventy	Seventy-six	Eighty

87	**90**	**98**
Eighty-seven	Ninety	Ninety-eight

100	**150**
One hundred	One hundred and fifty

4 *Open dialogue*

The customs officer is asking Janet questions. *What are they?*

OFFICER: ___ ___ suitcases ___ ___ ___?
JANET: Only two.
OFFICER: What ___ ___ ___ in them?
JANET: Well, I've got clothes in this suitcase and books in that one.
OFFICER: ___ ___ ___ whisky or cigarettes in them?
JANET: No, I haven't.

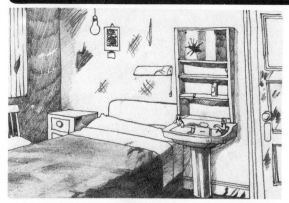

This is a room in "York House", a hotel in London.
It is a single. A single is a room with only one bed.
There is only one bed in this room.
There is a chair in the room, too. It is next to the window. And there is a washbasin next to the door.

And this is a room in "The Park Hotel". It is in London, too.
It is a double. A double is a room with two beds. There are two beds in this room.
There are two chairs in the room, too. The room has got a bathroom. There is a shower in the bathroom, and a toilet, too.

Terry Carter is in "York House".

TERRY: Have you got a room?
CLERK: A single? Or a double?
TERRY: A single, please.
CLERK: Yeah. I've got a single. £5 a night.
TERRY: £5? All right.
CLERK: Can you pay now?
TERRY: Yes. Here.

Janet is in "The Park Hotel".

CLERK: Good evening.
JANET: Good evening. My name is Snow. You've got a room reserved for me.
CLERK: Oh, yes, Miss Snow. Room four oh four. It's a double.
JANET: A double? With two beds?
CLERK: Yes. But the price is only for a single. Is that all right?
JANET: Yes, of course.

a

PICTURE ONE

1. Where is this room?
2. How many beds can you see?
3. Is the room a single?
4. What is a single?
5. What can you see in the room?
6. *Ask and answer*
   Is the ___ next to the ___?

PICTURE TWO

1. Is this a room in "York House"?
2. What can you see in it?
3. Is it a single or a double?
4. What is a double?
5. *Ask and answer*
   Has the room got ___ ___?

PICTURE THREE

1. Where is Terry now?
2. Is his room a single or a double?
3. How much is it?
4. Is Terry paying now?

PICTURE FOUR

1. Is Janet paying, too?
2. Where is she?
3. What is her room number?
4. Is it a single, too?
5. Is the price for a single?

b

1 (Stop and Look)

There	is	only one bed a chair	here. in this room.
	are	two beds three chairs	there.

2

There is   There are

There ___ one bed in his room. =
There is one bed in his room.
There ___ two beds in her room. =
There are two beds in her room.

1. There ___ one window in his room.
2. There ___ two windows in her room.
3. There ___ two chairs in her room, too.
4. But in his room there ___ only one chair.
5. There ___ twenty rooms in "York House".
6. And in "The Park Hotel" there ___ two hundred rooms.

3

This isn't a hotel room. It is a classroom.
What can you see in it?

How many	windows students teachers doors	are there in this classroom?

4

What about you?   *Speak about your classroom*

There $\begin{Bmatrix} is \\ are \end{Bmatrix}$ ___ ___ in my classroom.

C

🎧 *Listen to Janet and the clerk at "The Park Hotel"*

CLERK : How long are you staying, Miss Snow?
JANET : Three nights.
CLERK : Three nights. Thank you. Are those your suitcases?
JANET : Yes, they are.
CLERK : Porter! Those are Miss Snow's suitcases. Take them to room 404.
JANET : Thank you.
CLERK : Thank *you*, Miss Snow.
JANET : Oh. Where's the lift?
CLERK : It's on the left. The porter is going there now.

🎧 *Now listen to Terry and the clerk at "York House"*

CLERK : How long are you staying?
TERRY : Pardon? How long am I . . . what?
CLERK : How long are you staying? How many nights?
TERRY : Uh . . . one night. I'm staying one night.
CLERK : Oh. Here's your key. Room 16.
TERRY : Where is it?
CLERK : Four floors up.
TERRY : Is there a lift?
CLERK : A lift? No, there isn't.
TERRY : Oh. Where are the stairs?
CLERK : On the right.

3

How long is ___ staying?

Has ___ **got** a porter?

Is there a lift in ___?

4

You are in a hotel in London.

CLERK : What ___ ___ name, please?
YOU : ___ ___
CLERK : How ___ are you ___?
YOU : Two ___
CLERK : Thank you. ___ those your suitcases?
YOU : Yes, they ___
CLERK : Porter! Those are ___ ___'s suitcases. ___ them to ___ room.
YOU : Where's the ___?
CLERK : ___ ___ the right.

5

It is midnight.
Janet is in her hotel room.
She is writing a letter.

Terry is in bed.
He is reading a book.
There is a light over his bed.

Janet is speaking to the clerk on
the telephone.

JANET: This is room 404. Please
wake me at exactly seven
o'clock. Thank you.

It is seven in the morning now
and Janet's phone is ringing.
CLERK: It's seven o'clock, Miss
Snow. Good morning.

Terry's alarm clock is ringing. He
is getting up now, too.
He is tired.

And now it is seven thirty.
WAITER: Good morning,
madam. Here's your
breakfast. Bacon, eggs
and coffee. Is that all
right?

6 *Look at the answers.*
What are the questions?

1. Twelve o'clock midnight.
2. In her hotel room.
3. She is writing.
4. A letter.

5. He is in bed.
6. Yes, he is.
7. A book.
8. Over his bed.

9. She is speaking to the clerk.
10. No, he isn't in the room!

11. It is seven o'clock now.
12. No, not seven o'clock in the
    evening! Seven o'clock in the
    morning!

13. He is getting up.
14. No, his telephone isn't ringing.
    His alarm clock is!

WAITRESS: Here! Cornflakes,
toast and tea. OK?

1

Janet is standing at her window. What can she see?

This is Hyde Park. It is a big park in London. She can see Hyde Park from her window. Look at the trees. She can see them, too. She can see the buses and the cars in Park Lane. There's a policeman on a horse. She can see him, too.

What can Terry see from his window? Can he see Hyde Park? Can he see trees, buses or cars?

2

ASK and ANSWER

Can Janet **see** . . . ?
→ Yes, **she can.**/No, **she can't.**

Can Terry **see** . . . ?
→ Yes, **he can.**/No, **he can't.**

3

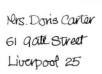

By Air Mail

Mr. H. Snow
4304 Grant Avenue
Westport
New York
U.S.A.

Dear Mum,
I'm in London now. I'm in a small hotel. Are you all right?
love,
Terry

Mrs. Doris Carter
61 Gate Street
Liverpool 25

Look at the letter and the postcard
The letter is from Janet to her father. He is in Westport, New York. Westport is near New York City.

The postcard is from Terry Carter to his mother. She is in Liverpool.
Can you see the stamp on Janet's letter? Is there a stamp on Terry's postcard?

Answer

1. Who is the letter from?
2. Who is it to?
3. Where is Westport?
4. Where is Janet's father?

5. Who is the postcard to?
6. Where is she?
7. Who is it from?
8. Where is he now?

e

1 It is nine o'clock in the morning now. Janet is in the hotel. *Listen*

CLERK: Good morning, Miss Snow.
JANET: Good morning. Can I buy a stamp here?
CLERK: For that letter?
JANET: Yes.
CLERK: Where's the letter going?
JANET: To New York.
CLERK: Airmail?
JANET: Yes.
CLERK: Eleven p, please.

2 And this is a post office. You can buy stamps in a post office. *Listen*

TERRY: A stamp for this postcard, please.
CLERK: Where's it going?
TERRY: Liverpool.
CLERK: Seven p, please.

3  Answer

1. What is Janet buying?
2. What is Terry buying?

3. Where is he buying it?
4. Where is she buying it?

5. How much is her stamp?
6. How much is his stamp?

4  Write

This is Janet's letter.

I ___ staying at "The Park Hotel".
= *I am staying at the Park Hotel.*

Thursday
September 1
Dear Dad,
I ___ staying at the Park Hotel in London.
___ is midnight and ___ am tired.
I ___ got ___ big room here and I ___ see Hyde Park ___ my window.
It ___ raining. I am going to bed in a minute.
Love,
Janet

5  **Open dialogues**

You are in a very small hotel in London.

YOU: ___ I ___ a stamp here?
CLERK: No, ___'m sorry. We ___ got stamps here.
YOU: Oh. Where ___ I ___ one?
CLERK: There's a ___ ___ near the hotel.
YOU: ___ is it?
CLERK: Two streets from here.
YOU: ___ you.

You are at the post office now.

YOU: Can I ___ a ___ for ___ letter?
CLERK: Where is ___ letter going?
YOU: To ___
CLERK: Airmail?
YOU: ___
CLERK: Eleven p, please.

FOR EXTRA PRACTICE, SEE READ AND WRITE 1, PAGE 107

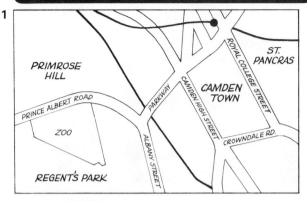

This is Camden Town. Camden Town is a part of London.
There is a big park in Camden Town. It is called Regent's Park. Can you see it on the map?

And this is Camden High Street. Look at the people, the cars and the shops.
Can you see that very big shop? It is a supermarket. You can buy food there – meat, vegetables, fruit and bread and things like that.

There is a cinema in Camden High Street. You can see films there. What is on today? Can you see?
"Texas Cowboy" is on. It is a western.
There is a pub next to the cinema. You can drink there.

And this is a travel agency in Camden Town. You can buy tickets here. Rail tickets and air tickets.
And you can get information here.

a

PICTURE ONE

1. What can you see in picture one?
2. Where is Camden Town?
3. What is there in Camden Town?

PICTURE TWO

1. What can you see in this picture?
2. What is that very big shop?
3. What can you buy there?

PICTURE THREE

1. Where is this cinema?
2. What is on today?
3. What is "Texas Cowboy"?

PICTURE FOUR

1. And what is this in picture four?
2. What can you buy here?
3. And what can you get?

1

The Camden English Centre is a school. You can learn English there. And Mike Sutton is a teacher at the Centre. He is teaching now. *Listen*

MIKE : Look at this man and this woman. His name is Wonderman and her name is Wonderwoman. He can fly and she can fly, too. He's very strong! He can lift a house. She's very strong, too, but she can't lift a house. But she can lift a car! And she's intelligent! She can speak ten foreign languages!

Wonderman isn't very intelligent. He can't speak any foreign languages. He can only speak English. That's all.

2

Can	Wonderman Wonderwoman	**fly**? **lift** a ___? **speak** ___?	→	Yes,	he she	**can.**
				No,	he she	**can't.**

3

Can you . . . ? → Yes, I can.
No, I can't.

C

1

 What are the people doing in these pictures?
Can you do these things very well?

1. George King is driving.
   Can you drive, too?

2. Janet is dancing.
   She can dance very well. What
   about you?

3. Terry is cooking, but he can't
   cook very well.

4. Mike is playing tennis.
   He can play tennis very well.

5. Anna is skiing.
   What about you?
   Can you ski, too?
   Can you ski very well?

6. Mike is swimming. But look at
   him! He can't swim very well!

2

Stop and Look

I/You He/She We/They	can	swim. dance. ski. drive.

Can	you he/she they	swim? dance? ski?

Now ask people in your class

Can you ___ ? → Yes, I can. No, I can't.
                  Yes, I can but not very well.

d

1

It is Friday, September 2nd (*the* second). Mary Norris is the manager of a travel agency in Camden Town. She is talking to Laura Francis. *Listen*

MARY: Can you type, Laura?
LAURA: Yes, I can.
MARY: How many words a minute?
LAURA: Eighty.
MARY: Hmm. And can you speak any foreign languages?
LAURA: Yes, I can. I can speak French. And I can speak German.
MARY: Really? That's very good! What about Spanish?
LAURA: No, I can't speak Spanish. But I can speak Italian. But not very well.
MARY: Hmm. Can you start next month?
LAURA: Start next month?
MARY: Yes. In October.
LAURA: You mean, I've got the job?
MARY: Yes, that's right. You've got the job!

2

Can Laura . . . ?
How many ___s can she ___?

3

Can you . . . ?
How many ___ can you ___?

Now speak and write about Laura

1. She ___ ___ eighty words a minute.
2. She ___ ___ French and German.
3. She ___ ___ Spanish but she ___ ___ Italian.

5

What about you?

I can/I can't

Can you speak any foreign languages? Can you type? How many words a minute? Can you swim? Can you drive? Can you ski or play tennis? What can you do?

1

This is a bedsitter in Camden Town. A bedsitter is one room. You can sleep in it and you can sit in it.

There is a bed in the room and there are two chairs and a table, too. Can you see them?

And there's a small fire in the room. Can you see it, too?

Terry Carter is looking for a room like this.

2

This is a flat. There are four rooms in the flat. One room is the kitchen. There is a cooker and a fridge in the kitchen. One room is the living room. One room is the bedroom. And one room is the bathroom. There is a toilet and a shower in the bathroom. But which room is the kitchen? Which room is the bathroom? Which room is the living room? And which room is the bedroom?

There are two tables in the living room. Can you see them?

Janet Snow is looking for a flat like this.

3

Is there a ___ in the ___?   **How many** ___s **are there** in the ___? **Where** is the ___?

Now speak about your room or flat

There is/are ___ in my flat.   **I've got/I haven't got** a ___ in my ___

f

1

Terry Carter is phoning about the bedsitter. He is talking to a woman called Mrs Jason. *Listen*

MRS JASON: Five nine seven, three oh four eight. Hello?

TERRY: Hello. I'm phoning about the bedsitter.

MRS JASON: Oh yes.

TERRY: Can you tell me about it, please. I mean, what's in the room?

MRS JASON: Well, there's a bed in it, of course. And there are two chairs and . . . uh . . . there's a table in it and . . .

TERRY: And where is it? What's your address, I mean.

MRS JASON: Sixty-four Marston Street. We're very near Camden High Street.

TERRY: Ahh. And how much is the rent, please?

MRS JASON: The rent? Fifteen pounds a week.

TERRY: Can I see the room, please?

MRS JASON: Yes, of course. Can you come now?

TERRY: Yes. I'm coming now. In five or ten minutes. Is that all right?

MRS JASON: Yes, of course.

TERRY: Goodbye.

MRS JASON: Goodbye. Oh! Wait! What's your name, please?

TERRY: Carter.

MRS JASON: Can you spell it, please?

TERRY: C __ A __ R __ T __ E __ R.

MRS JASON: Thank you, Mr Carter. See you in five or ten minutes.

2

Open dialogues

And now Janet is phoning about the flat. She is talking to a man called Young. What is she saying?

MR YOUNG: Hello?

JANET: ___ ___ ___ the flat. ___ ___ tell ___ ___ it?

MR YOUNG: Yes, of course. What can I tell you about it?

JANET: Well, ___ many rooms ___ there in ___ flat?

MR YOUNG: There are four rooms: a bedroom, a living room, a kitchen and a bathroom of course.

JANET: ___ ___ ___?

MR YOUNG: It's in Camden Town, very near Regent's Park.

JANET: ___ ___ ___?

MR YOUNG: Fifty-eight Albert Gardens. That's a street, of course.

JANET: ___ ___ ___ ___ ___?

MR YOUNG: Two hundred pounds a month.

JANET: ___ ___ ___ ___ ___?

MR YOUNG: Yes, of course. Can you come now?

JANET: Yes. I'm ___ in thirty ___ forty minutes. ___ ___ all right?

MR YOUNG: Yes, of course.

JANET: ___ ___

MR YOUNG: Goodbye.

3

Write

Write about the flat

flat/near Regent's Park.
= *The flat is near Regent's Park.*

1. four rooms/the flat
2. rent/£200 a month
3. two windows/living room
4. a shower/bathroom
5. address/58 Albert Gardens

It is Monday morning, October 3rd (*the* third). It is seven in the morning. The sun is shining. Can you see that big block of flats? It is very near Regent's Park.

Janet Snow lives there now. She lives in a flat near Regent's Park.

Her address is 58 Albert Gardens, LONDON NW 3.

Mary Norris is getting up. The man in bed is her husband. His name is Peter Norris. Mary and Peter are married. They live in the same block of flats. Their address is 58 Albert Gardens, too.

MARY: Come on, Peter. Get up. It's seven o'clock. The sun's shining.

PETER: Oh . . . no! Turn on the radio, please.

What's on the radio this morning?
Marty Davis is on. He is a disc jockey. His programme is starting.

MARTY: Hi, everybody. This is Marty Davis with your programme of records and music this morning. And here's our first record this morning. It's called "Hello, Sun".

But Janet can't hear Marty. She isn't listening to him now. She is running in Regent's Park. And a man is watching her. He can see her. But she can't see him. He is standing behind a tree.

a

PICTURE ONE

1. Is it September now?
2. What month is it?
3. What can you see in the first picture?
4. What is Janet's address now?

PICTURE TWO

1. What can you see in the second picture?
2. *Speak about Mary and Peter*
   They ___ married.
   They ___ in a flat.

PICTURE THREE

1. What can you see in the third picture?
2. Who is Marty Davis?
3. What is the first record this morning?

PICTURE FOUR

1. What can you see in the fourth picture?
2. *Speak about Janet*
   She ___ running.
   She ___ in a flat.
3. *Speak about the man*
   Where is he?
   What is he doing?

b

1

Say **That's right.**
That's wrong.

Janet Snow and Peter Norris are married. = **That's wrong.**
Mary and Peter Norris are married. =   **That's right.**

1. Janet lives near Regent's Park.
2. Mary and Peter live near Regent's Park, too.
3. They live in a house.
4. They live in a flat.
5. Janet lives in a house.
6. Marty Davis is listening to Janet.
7. She is listening to him.
8. Mary and Peter are listening to him.
9. Janet is running and a man is watching her.

2   **Stop and Look**

He She	lives		
		in	a house. a flat. London. England.
I We You They	live		

3
Speak and Write

 Mike Sutton

1. He ___ in a flat.
2. ___ address ___
   18 Egbert Street,
   LONDON NW 3.

 Anna Parker

1. She ___ a flat, too.
2. ___ address ___
   22 Manley Street,
   LONDON NW 3.

 Terry Carter

1. ___ ___ ___ a bedsitter.
2. ___ address ___
   64 Marston Street,
   LONDON NW 3.

What about you?

1. I ___ ___ house/flat/ bedsitter.
2. ___ address ___
   . . .

1

It is eight fifteen now. Mary and Peter Norris are leaving their flat now. The boy with them is Simon, their son. And that man is a postman.

POSTMAN: Excuse me. Do you live here?

MARY: Yes, we do. We live on the third floor.

POSTMAN: Oh. Does Janet Snow live here, too?

MARY: Who? Janet Snow? Do you know that name, Peter?

PETER: Janet Snow? No, I don't. I'm sorry.

SIMON: I know her!

PETER: Do you? Well? Does she live here?

SIMON: Yes, she does. She's an American! She lives under us. She lives in the flat on the second floor!

POSTMAN: Oh. Thanks! I've got a letter for her but I can't see her name on the postbox.

2 *Look at these questions and answers again*

Does $\begin{Bmatrix} \text{Janet Snow} \\ \text{Terry Carter} \end{Bmatrix}$ **live** here? →
Yes, $\begin{Bmatrix} \text{she} \\ \text{he} \end{Bmatrix}$ **does**.

No, $\begin{Bmatrix} \text{she} \\ \text{he} \end{Bmatrix}$ **doesn't**.

Can you answer the questions now?

1. Does Mary Norris live in a flat?
2. Does Peter live in a flat, too?
3. Does Simon live there?
4. Does Janet live in a flat, too?
5. Does Peter know her name?
6. Does Mary know her?
7. Does Simon know her?
8. Does Janet live on the third floor?
9. Does Simon live on the second floor?

3 (*Stop and Look*)

Do you **live** here? → Yes, I **do**.

Do you **know** Janet Snow? No, I **don't**.

4

What about you?

1. Do you live near Regent's Park?
2. Do you live in Camden Town?
3. Do you live in London?
4. Do you live in a city?
5. Do you live near a city?
6. Do you live in a house?
7. Do you live in a flat?
8. Do you live near a park?

c

5 **Open dialogues**

You are talking to Terry Carter. Terry lives in a bedsitter in Camden Town.

What are your questions?
What are his answers?

YOU: ___ you ___ ___ Camden Town?
TERRY: ___, ___ ___
YOU: ___ ___ ___ ___ ___ flat?
TERRY: ___, ___ ___
      I ___ ___ ___ bedsitter.

And now George is speaking to Lucky. He's asking questions about Janet Snow.

GEORGE: ___ she ___ in Camden Town?
LUCKY: Yes, ___ ___
GEORGE: ___ ___ ___ ___ ___ house?
LUCKY: No, ___ ___. She ___ ___ ___ flat.

d

1 Where do they work?

Mary Norris works in a travel agency.
She is the manager. Laura Francis works there, too.
Mary is Laura's boss.

Peter Norris works in a factory.
He is an engineer.

And now listen to Anna Parker and Mike Sutton

ANNA: I work in an office. I'm not a secretary. I'm a newspaper reporter. I work for "The Camden Times". It is a small newspaper in Camden Town.

MIKE: And me? I'm a teacher. I work in the Camden English Centre. I teach English there.

2 ASK and ANSWER

Does	Mary Laura Peter Mike Anna	work in	a ___? an ___?
		teach	English?

3 Ask people in your class

Do you { work / live } in { a ___?
an ___? }

1

And this is Laura Francis again.
What about her?

Laura is single. She lives in a house in Watford.
Watford is a town near London.
Laura lives with her father. Her mother is dead.

2

Laura is going to work now. She has got a new job
in a travel agency in Camden Town. It is her first
day today.

LAURA: Dad! I'm going to work now.
MR FRANCIS: Oh! Goodbye, Laura.
LAURA: See you this evening.
MR FRANCIS: Yes. Bye!

3

Laura is waiting for her train now. She is at Watford
Station. She can see a friend. Her friend works in
London, too.

LAURA: Hello, Jenny! How are you?
JENNY: Fine, thanks. How are you?
LAURA: Fine, thanks. Are you going to work?
JENNY: Yes, I am. And you?
LAURA: Yes. I've got a new job in Camden Town!

4

And now Laura is in the travel agency. Mary Norris
is her boss. The man and the other woman work
there, too.

MARY: Laura! This is Betty Jensen. Betty! This is
        Laura Francis.
LAURA: Hello!
BETTY: Hello!
MARY: And this is David Stone.
DAVID: How do you do?
LAURA: Hello. Pleased to meet you.

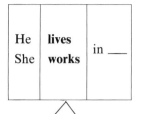

What are the questions?
What are the answers?

PICTURE ONE

1. ___ Laura live in Camden Town?
No, ___ ___
2. ___ she ___ in Watford?
Yes, ___ ___

PICTURE TWO

1. ___ Laura going to work now?
___, ___ ___
2. Is her father ___ to work, too?
No, ___ ___

PICTURE THREE

1. Where ___ Laura now?
She ___ at ___ ___
2. ___ she see a friend?
Yes, ___ ___
3. ___ her friend ___ to work?
Yes, she ___
4. Does she ___ in London?
Yes, ___ ___

PICTURE FOUR

1. ___ Betty Jensen Laura's boss?
No, ___ ___
2. ___ Betty work in a travel agency?
___, ___ ___
3. ___ David Stone ___ there, too? ___, ___ ___

f

1 Stop and Look

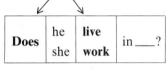

He / She	lives / works	in ___

I / You / They / We	live / work	in ___

Does	he / she	live / work	in ___?

Do	you / they	live / work	in ___?

→ Yes, {he / she} **does.**

No, {he / she} **doesn't.**

Yes, {I / we / they} **do.**

No, {I / we / they} **don't.**

2 Open dialogue

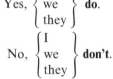

David Stone is speaking to Laura Francis. It is one o'clock. They are having lunch.

DAVID: ___ you ___ in Camden Town, Laura?
LAURA: No, ___ ___. I ___ ___ Watford.
DAVID: Oh. ___ you married?
LAURA: No, ___ ___. But I ___ with a man.
DAVID: What? Oh, really?
LAURA: Yes, ___ ___ with ___ father.

3 Write

This is a letter from Janet to her father. *Tuesday October 4*

___ Dad,

I ___ in Camden Town now. ___ got a very nice flat here. I ___ see Regent's Park ___ my window.

I've got ___ friend here, too! ___ name is Simon Norris. I ___ ___ the second ___ and he ___. ___ the ___ floor. ___ is only ___ boy!

His father ___ in a factory and ___ mother ___ in a travel agency.

40

This is Janet Snow again. You know this about her:
She lives in Camden Town. She is from New York. But you don't know this about her:
She is a student in London. She goes to the London School of Dance. Her father lives in New York. He is very rich. He is the president of a bank.

It is Friday, November 4th (the fourth) now and it is seven o'clock in the morning. Janet is getting up. She always gets up at seven o'clock in the morning. She always runs in Regent's Park. She runs there every morning, seven days a week.

It is seven thirty now and she is having breakfast. She is listening to Marty Davis's programme. It always starts at seven o'clock. And Janet always has breakfast at seven thirty. She always listens to him.

MARTY: Hi, everybody. You're listening to Marty Davis. It's seven thirty. Are you getting up?

It is nine o'clock now. Janet is leaving her flat. She always leaves the flat at nine. And Marty's programme is finishing. It always finishes at nine.

MARTY: Well, that's all for this morning. Bye!

a

PICTURE ONE

What are the questions and answers?

1. Where ___ Janet live?
2. ___ her father ___ in London, too?
3. Where ___ he live?
4. ___ he rich?
5. ___ Janet go to the London School of Dance?

PICTURE TWO

Answer the questions

1. Is Janet running now?
2. Is she getting up?
3. What time is it?
4. What time does she get up in the morning?
5. What about you? What time do you get up?

PICTURE THREE

Speak about Janet

1. She is . . .
2. She always . . .

Ask questions

3. Is Janet . . . ?
4. Does she always . . . ?

PICTURE FOUR

Answer the questions

1. Is she listening to the radio now?
2. Is the programme starting?
3. Is it finishing?
4. What time does it start?
5. What time does it finish?

b

1 (Stop and Say)

lives   starts   finishes

1. Janet **lives** in London now.
2. The radio programme **starts** at seven thirty.
3. It **finishes** at nine.

2 This is Terry Carter again. Do you remember him? *Listen to him*

TERRY: I live in a small bedsitter in Camden Town. I get up at seven or at eight. Sometimes I get up at nine.

I have breakfast at seven thirty or at eight thirty. And sometimes I don't have breakfast at all.

I'm a student, too. But I don't go to the London School of Dance. I go to London University.

3

Speak and write about Janet and Terry

1. **He lives in a ___ and she . . .**
2. **She gets up at ___ and he . . .**
3. **She ___ breakfast at ___ and he . . .**
4. **She goes to the ___ and he . . .**

4

What about you?

1. **I live . . .**
2. **I get up at . . .**
3. **I have breakfast at . . .**
4. **I leave my flat/house at . . .**
5. **I start school/work at . . . and I finish at . . .**

C

Do you remember George King? He is speaking to Lucky Jones. And they are speaking about Janet.

Listen

GEORGE: All right, Lucky. You watch this girl every day. When does she leave her flat in the morning?

LUCKY: She leaves at nine.

GEORGE: Every morning?

LUCKY: No. Not on Saturday or Sunday.

GEORGE: Hmm. When does she have lunch?

LUCKY: Usually at one.

GEORGE: Usually? Not always?

LUCKY: No. Sometimes she doesn't have lunch at all.

GEORGE: Hmm. And where does she have lunch?

LUCKY: Sometimes in a restaurant near the school. And sometimes in the school canteen.

GEORGE: I see. Now, what does she do in the evening?

LUCKY: She usually gets home at five or at five thirty. I think she usually has dinner at six.

GEORGE: You *think*? Do you *know*?

LUCKY: No, I don't. And I think she often watches television. I know she sometimes goes to a pub in Camden Town.

GEORGE: A pub? Which pub?

LUCKY: "The Bell". It's in Camden High Street. She goes there with some friends.

GEORGE: Some friends? Which friends?

LUCKY: I don't know their names.

2

Look again at this question

When (What time) does Janet leave her flat?
She leaves **at nine**.

Now answer these questions

1. When does she have lunch?
2. Does she always have lunch at one?
3. When does she get home?
4. When does she have dinner?
5. Does Lucky know this? Or does he think this?
6. When does she watch television?
7. Where does she sometimes go in the evening?

3 Ask people in your class . . .

When do you	get up?
	have breakfast?
	go to work/school?
	have lunch/dinner?
	get home?
	go to bed?

4

What about you?

I	**always** **usually** **sometimes**	get up leave home ___ to school/work ___ lunch ___ home ___ to bed	at ___

d

1

It is eight o'clock in the evening now. Janet is sitting in her flat. She often watches television in the evening. Can you see the stereo and the records? She often listens to records, too.

There are some books in that bookcase. She often reads in the evening.

What is she doing now?

Terry is sitting on the floor of his bedsitter. He never watches television. He hasn't got a television set. And he hasn't got a stereo or records. But he often listens to the radio.

Sometimes he reads books, too. There are some books on the table. Can you see them?

Terry isn't a very good student.

Terry often plays his guitar in "The Bell". He sings, too. What is he doing now?

2

Look at these questions and answers

Is Janet **listening** to the radio now?
No, she **isn't**.

Does she **listen** to the radio in the evening?
Yes, she **does**.

3

Can you ask and answer these?

1. ___ she sitting in her flat?
   Yes, she ___
2. ___ she listen to records in the evening?
   Yes, she ___
3. Does she ___ television, too?
   ___, she ___
4. Is she ___ television now?
   Yes, she ___

4

Now ask some questions about Terry.
What are the answers?

Does he . . . in the evening?
Is he ___ing now?

5

What about you?

What do you do in the evening?

I	**often**	___ television.
	never	___ to a pub.
	sometimes	___ to the radio.
	usually	___ to records.
	always	___ books.
		___ the guitar.

1

It is nine thirty and Janet is in "The Bell" with Mike and Anna. Mike and Anna are her friends. Terry is playing his guitar. He is finishing now.

ANNA: Hmm. Very good. He plays very well.
JANET: Yes, I think so, too. What's his name?
ANNA: I don't know. Mike! Do you know him?
MIKE: Yes, I do. His name's Terry Carter. He's a student. He often plays the guitar here.
JANET: Really? When?
MIKE: Well, usually on Wednesday and Friday.
JANET: Oh.
ANNA: He's coming over here now.
MIKE: Terry! How are you this evening?
TERRY: Oh, hello, Mike. How are you?
MIKE: Fine, thanks. Oh. Terry. This is Anna Parker. And this is Janet Snow.
ANNA: Hello, Terry. Nice to meet you.
TERRY: Hello. And . . . pardon . . . what's your name?
JANET: Janet. Janet Snow.
TERRY: Nice to meet you. Erm . . . do you often come here?
JANET: No. Not often. Sometimes.
TERRY: Oh? When?
JANET: Usually on Saturdays.
TERRY: Oh? Really? Erm . . . cigarette?
JANET: No thanks. I don't smoke.

2

Does ___ know ___ ?
When does . . . ?
Does ___ **think** Terry plays well?

3

Speak about the conversation, like this

. . . **knows** . . . but . . . **doesn't know** . . .
. . . **often** . . .
. . . **comes** to "The Bell" on . . .

4

You are speaking to Mike in "The Bell".
What are his questions? What are your answers?

MIKE: ___ ___ name?
YOU: ___ ___
MIKE: Where ___ ___ ___ from?
YOU: ___ ___ ___ ___
MIKE: Oh! ___ is Janet Snow and Anna Parker.
YOU: Nice ___ ___ ___
MIKE: ___ you often ___ here?
YOU: ___ ___ ___

5

her   him   them

Mike knows Anna. = *He knows her.*

1. Janet knows Mike. ___ knows ___
2. Terry knows Mike. ___ knows ___
3. Anna knows Janet.
4. Janet knows Anna and Mike.
5. George knows Janet.
6. Janet doesn't know George.

f

	He She	**lives** in Camden Town. **works** in an office. **watches** television in the evening. **goes** to a school in London. **plays** the guitar. **smokes** English cigarettes.		I We They You	**live** in ___ **work** in ___ **watch** television in the evening, too. **go** to a school in ___ **play** the ___ **smoke** ___ cigarettes.

Does	he she	**live** in ___ ?	→	Yes,	he she	**does**.		No,	he she	**doesn't**.
Do	I we they you	**go** to ___ ? **work** in ___ ? **smoke** ___ ? etc.			I we they you	**do**.			I we they you	**don't**.

2

What is Mike saying?

I ___ in a flat in Camden Town. ___ address ___ 18 Egbert Street. ___ ___ English in the Camden English Centre.
___ usually ___ breakfast ___ 8 in the morning. And ___ ___ lunch ___ 12 or 1 o'clock ___ ___ small restaurant ___ school.
___ ___ evening ___ often ___ television or ___ to the radio. ___ Wednesday and Friday ___ usually ___ to "The Bell". ___ Saturday ___ often ___ to the cinema ___ Anna Parker.

3

What about you?

I live/work in . . .
___ go to . . .
___ usually get up at . . .
___ ___ breakfast at . . .
In the evening I often/usually . . .

4

Write about Mike

He lives . . . teaches . . . He often/usually . . .
On Wednesday and Friday he . . . etc.

5

Here are some questions about Mike.
What are they? What are the answers?

1. ___ he ___ English? Yes, ___ ___
2. ___ he usually ___ breakfast at ___? ___, he ___
3. When ___ he usually ___ lunch? At ___ ___ ___ ___
4. Where ___ he usually ___ lunch?
   ___ ___ ___ ___
5. ___ he often ___ television in the ___? Yes, ___ ___

6

Mike is asking you questions! What are they and what are the answers?

1. Where ___ you live? I ___ ___ ___
2. ___ you work ___ a factory? ___, ___ ___
3. ___ you ___ to London University? ___, ___ ___
4. When ___ you ___ up in the morning?
   I usually ___ ___ at ___ ___
5. ___ you often ___ television ___ ___ evening?
   ___, ___ ___

FOR EXTRA PRACTICE, SEE READ AND WRITE 2, PAGE 109

It is Friday, December 9th (*the* ninth).
It is exactly twelve noon.
Peter Norris works in a factory. He is having lunch in the factory canteen.
His wife, Mary, doesn't work in a factory.
She works in a travel agency.
She isn't having lunch. She is dictating a letter to her secretary.

Janet Snow goes to the London School of Dance.
She is practising now. One of her teachers is watching her.
Terry Carter doesn't go to the London School of Dance. He goes to London University. He is listening to a lecture now.

Anna Parker works for a newspaper.
She is writing an article now.
Mike Sutton doesn't work for a newspaper.
He teaches English.
He is teaching now. The lesson starts at 11.45 and finishes at 12.30.

Mike lives in a flat near the school.
There is a man in the flat now.
The man doesn't live in the flat and Mike doesn't know him.
The man is a burglar and he is stealing things from Mike's flat.

a

PICTURES ONE, TWO AND THREE

Look at this question and answer

What **is** Peter **doing** now?
→ He **is having** lunch.

Now ask and answer

What **is** ⎰Mary
Janet
Terry
Anna
Mike⎱ **doing**?

→ He
She ⎱ **is** ___ **ing**.

Now ask and answer

Does	Peter Mary Janet Anna Terry Mike	**work** in ___ ? **teach** ___? **go** to ___? **work** for ___?

→ Yes, ___ **does**.
No, ___ **doesn't**.

PICTURE FOUR

1. Who is this man?
2. Where is he?
3. What is he doing?
4. Does he live in the flat?
5. Can Mike see him?
6. Does Mike know him?

1

These things are wrong.
Answer like this

Terry **works** in a factory.
= No, that's wrong. He **doesn't work** in a factory.

1. Peter works in a travel agency.
2. Mary works in a factory.
3. Janet goes to London University.
4. Terry goes to the London School of Dance.
5. Anna Parker teaches English.
6. Mike Sutton works for a newspaper.
7. The burglar lives in Mike's flat.
8. Mike knows the burglar.

2

Do you remember Laura Francis?
Do you remember these things about her?

Laura lives in a house.
She lives in Watford.
Watford is a town near London.

Laura works in London.
She works in a travel agency in Camden Town.
Mary Norris is her boss.
Laura starts at nine every morning and finishes at five thirty.
She goes to work on the train.
She goes home on the train, too.

Where . . . ? Does . . . ? Is . . . ?

3

1. Laura doesn't ___ in a factory and she ___ teach English.
2. She doesn't ___ in a flat and she ___ live in Camden Town.

1

But what about the burglar in Mike Sutton's flat?

A man can see him. The man's name is Mr Benson and he lives across the street. He lives in a flat on the fourth floor. Mike lives in a flat on the third floor.

Mr Benson is phoning the police. *Listen*

MR BENSON:	There's a burglar in the flat.
POLICEMAN:	In which flat? In your flat?
MR BENSON:	No! I don't live in the flat. I mean, there isn't a burglar in my flat but in Mr Sutton's flat. I can see him now.
POLICEMAN:	Who? Mr Sutton?
MR BENSON:	No, you don't understand! I can't see Mr Sutton! I can see a man in his flat. I can see him through the window.
POLICEMAN:	And the man isn't Mr Sutton?
MR BENSON:	No, he isn't.
POLICEMAN:	Are you sure?
MR BENSON:	Yes, of course I am! I know Mr Sutton! But I don't know the man in his flat! I'm sure he's a burglar! Come now! Hurry! Do you understand? I'm sure there's a burglar in Mr Sutton's flat!

2 *Answer*

1. Where does Mr Benson live?
2. What can he see?
3. Who is he phoning?
4. What is he saying about the man in Mike's flat?
5. Who does he know? Who doesn't he know?

3

These things are wrong.
Answer like this

Mr Benson **is** a burglar.
→ No! He **isn't** a burglar.

He **knows** the burglar.
→ No! He **doesn't know** the burglar.

1. Mr Benson lives in Mike's flat.
2. He can see Mike.
3. He is phoning Mike.
4. He knows the man in Mike's flat.
5. The policeman understands.
6. Mr Benson is a policeman.
7. The policeman knows the burglar.
8. The policeman works in a travel agency.
9. The burglar works for a newspaper.
10. He teaches English in Mike's school.
11. The burglar can hear Mr Benson.
12. The burglar is a policeman.

4 *Speak and Write*

1. Mr Benson lives . . .
2. He can see a ___ in ___ ___
3. He is phoning ___ ___
4. He knows ___ ___ but he doesn't know ___ ___
5. He is sure . . .

d

1

It is two o'clock in the afternoon now and the police have got the burglar. They are asking him questions.

POLICEMAN: All right, what's your name?

FRANK: Frank.

POLICEWOMAN: Frank what? What's your last name?

FRANK: Mitchum.

POLICEMAN: Spell it.

FRANK: F __ R __ A __

POLICEMAN: No! Not your Christian name! Spell your last name!

FRANK: M __ I __ T __ C __ H __ U __ M.

POLICEWOMAN: Where are you from, Frank?

FRANK: Manchester. But I don't live there.

POLICEMAN: Where *do* you live?

FRANK: Here. In Camden Town. In a bedsitter.

POLICEWOMAN: Give us the address, please.

FRANK: 43 Weston Street. W __ E __ S __ T __ O __ N.

POLICEMAN: Have you got a job?

FRANK: No, I haven't. I don't work. I can't find a job.

POLICEWOMAN: Hmm. Tell us about your parents, Frank. Your mother and father.

FRANK: I don't live with them.

POLICEWOMAN: Where do they live?

FRANK: My mother lives in Manchester.

POLICEWOMAN: And your father?

FRANK: I don't know. I think he lives in Liverpool. But I'm not sure.

POLICEMAN: OK. That's all for now. No more questions now. Take him away!

2

Ask and answer questions about the burglar

Does he $\left\{\begin{array}{l}\text{live}\\\text{work}\end{array}\right\}$ in ___?

Where does his $\left\{\begin{array}{l}\text{mother}\\\text{father}\end{array}\right\}$ ___?

Is he sure $\left\{\begin{array}{l}\text{his father}\\\text{his mother}\end{array}\right\}$ lives in ___?

3

Speak and write about the burglar

1. ___ name ___ ___ ___
2. ___ ___ from ___
3. He ___ live in Manchester.
4. His mother ___ in ___
5. He doesn't ___ with her.
6. ___ thinks ___ father ___ in Liverpool but ___ ___ sure.
7. ___ address ___ 43 Weston Street.
8. ___ ___ ___ a bedsitter.
9. He ___ ___ a job.
10. He ___ work.

1

Here is George King again. What do you know about him? And what don't you know about him?

George doesn't work in a travel agency or a factory. He has got a nightclub. It is called "The King Club". George owns it. It is his nightclub.

He doesn't live in a flat or a bedsitter. He lives in a big house. He owns a big car. He smokes big cigars. And he smokes a lot of cigars. He smokes 20 cigars a day. He earns a lot of money, too. He earns £40,000 a year. That is a lot of money but George wants more! He wants more money.

He is looking at a photograph of Janet Snow. She doesn't know him. But he knows her. Janet's father is very rich. He knows that, too.

2

We can say about George:
"**He doesn't work** in a factory."
But George says:
"**I don't work** in a factory."

What is George saying now?

1. He doesn't live in a flat.
2. He doesn't smoke cigarettes.
3. He doesn't smoke small cigars.
4. He doesn't get up at seven.
5. He doesn't run in Regent's Park.
6. He doesn't teach English.
7. He doesn't know Mike Sutton.
8. He doesn't watch television every evening.

3

What about you?

Are these things right or wrong?

You own a nightclub. = That's right. I **own** a nightclub.

or

That's wrong. I **don't own** a night-club.

1. You work in a nightclub, too.
2. You smoke 40 cigars a day.
3. You earn £100,000 a year.
4. You steal things from houses.
5. You go to London University.
6. You own four cars.
7. You understand ten foreign languages.
8. You live in a bedsitter in Camden Town.
9. You go to "The Bell" every evening.

f

Stop and Look

George	owns lives earns drinks smokes	a nightclub. in a big house. £40,000 a year. whisky every day. big cigars.

Mike Terry I	doesn't	own live	a nightclub. in a big house.
You We They	don't	earn drink smoke	£40,000 a year. whisky every day. big cigars.

2

Write about George King

1. George ___ a nightclub.
2. He ___ a big car.
3. He ___ in ___ big house.
4. He ___ rich.
5. He ___ £40,000 a year.

3

Do you remember Laura Francis?
Can you write about her?

1. She d___ o___ a nightclub.
2. She ___n't ___ a big car.
3. She d___ l___ in London.
4. Laura l___ in Watford.
5. She d___ w___ in a nightclub.
6. She ___ in a travel agency.

4

Here are Peter and Mary Norris again.
Do you remember them?

1. They d___ l___ in Watford.
2. They l___ in a flat in Camden Town.
3. They d___ o___ a nightclub.
4. Peter w___ in a factory but he d___ e___ £40,000 a year.
5. He ___ £7,000 a year.
6. Mary ___ in a travel agency and ___ £5,000 a year.

5

What is Mike Sutton saying?

1. I d___ ___ a nightclub and I d___ ___ £40,000 a year.
2. I ___ £5,000 a year.
3. I ___n't ___ a big car.
4. I d___ ___ big cigars and I d___ ___ three bottles of whisky a week!

6

Peter and Mary Norris are talking.
What are they saying?

1. We d___ l___ in a big house.
2. We l___ in a flat in Camden Town.
3. We ___n't ___ a big car.
4. We d___ s___ cigars or cigarettes.

1

Do you remember Tracey? It is January now and it is very cold. Tracey is in a café. He wants a cup of tea. And he can pay for it. His money is in his hand.

TRACEY: A cup of tea, please.
WAITER: Can you pay for it?
TRACEY: Of course I can! Here's my money! Look!

2

Frank Mitchum is in prison now. He doesn't like it. And he doesn't like the food.

FRANK: This food is terrible!
PRISONER: Can I have it? I'm hungry.
FRANK: Here, take it! I don't want it!

3

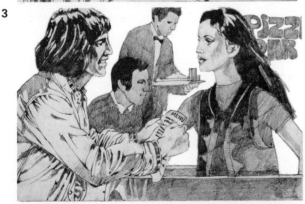

Terry and Janet are having dinner in an Italian restaurant.

TERRY: Do you like pizza?
JANET: Yes, I do. Very much. I often have it.
TERRY: Well, there are ten kinds of pizza here. What kind do you want?
JANET: Hmm. Let's see. The second, I think. With salami. What about you?
TERRY: Uh . . . the same for me.

4

Peter and Mary Norris are having dinner at home. They are having steak and salad. But Peter isn't very hungry.

MARY: What's wrong? Don't you like the steak?
PETER: Yes, I do. But I'm not very hungry. I can't really eat it. Here. You take it.
MARY: All right.

PICTURE ONE

1. Where is Tracey?
2. What has he got in his hand?
3. He wants a cup of tea. What is he saying?
4. What is the waiter's question?
5. What is Tracey's answer?

PICTURE TWO

1. Where is Frank?
2. What is he doing?
3. What is he saying?
4. Does he like the food?
5. Does he like the prison?
6. Look at the other man. Does he want Frank's food?

PICTURE THREE

1. Where are Terry and Janet?
2. Does Janet like pizza?
3. Which pizza does she want?
4. What about Terry?

PICTURE FOUR

1. What are Mary and Peter doing?
2. Is Peter hungry?
3. Does he like steak?
4. Does he want it now?
5. Does Mary want it?

b

1 (Stop and Look)

He She	wants likes doesn't like	a cup of tea. pizza. steak.

(a) Terry is saying: "This pizza is good."
You can say: **He likes the pizza.**

Terry is saying: "This pizza is terrible!"
You can say: **He doesn't like the pizza.**

What can you say now?

1. Janet is saying: "This pizza is very good."
2. Frank is saying: "This food is terrible!"
3. Mary is saying: "This steak is very good!"
4. Peter is saying: "This salad isn't very good."

(b) Tracey is saying: "A cup of tea, please."
You can say: **He wants a cup of tea.**

What can you say now?

1. Tracey is saying: "A sandwich, please."
2. Terry is saying to the waiter: "A pizza, please."
3. Janet is saying: "A pizza for me, too, please."
4. Terry is saying: "And two cups of coffee, please."

2

Janet is talking about what she likes for breakfast in the morning. *Listen*

JANET: I usually have a cup of coffee, and a grapefruit. I like grapefruit in the morning. I often have an egg, too. And I like toast with marmalade.

3

What about you?

What do you like for { breakfast? lunch? dinner? }

I { **often** **sometimes** } have . . . I like . . .

54

1 🔊 *Look at the pictures. Do you know what these things are?*

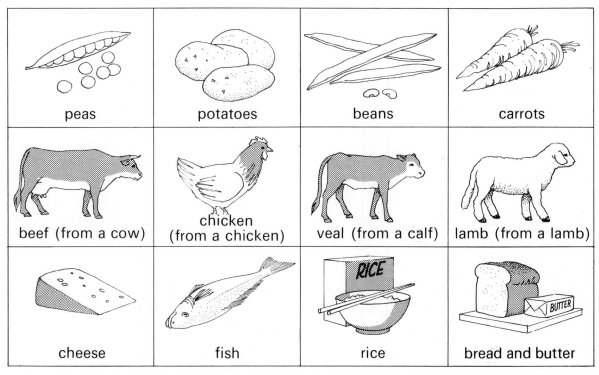

peas	potatoes	beans	carrots
beef (from a cow)	chicken (from a chicken)	veal (from a calf)	lamb (from a lamb)
cheese	fish	rice	bread and butter

You can see four kinds of vegetable here. And you can see four kinds of meat, too. Meat comes from animals. The name of the animal and the name of the meat aren't always the same.

Look at the last four pictures, too. These things aren't meat. But they aren't vegetables, either!

2 **? Ask people in your class ...**

Do you like ___?
Do you often eat ___?

3 **What about you?**

I like ___. I don't like ___
I often eat ___. I never eat ___
Sometimes I eat ___

4

And how do you like these things? Answer like this

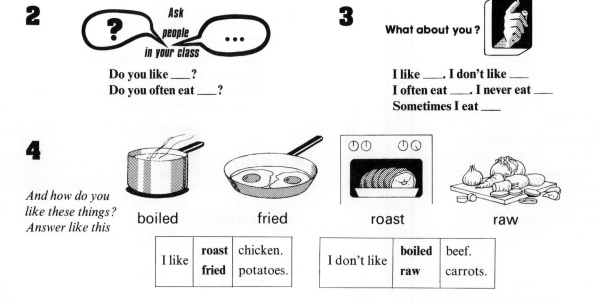

boiled   fried   roast   raw

| I like | **roast** | chicken. |
| | **fried** | potatoes. |

| I don't like | **boiled** | beef. |
| | **raw** | carrots. |

d

1

Janet and Terry want to go to the cinema. The film starts at eight thirty. It is seven forty-five now and they are in an Italian restaurant.

WAITER: Can I have your order, please?

TERRY: Two pizzas with salami, please.

WAITER: And to drink? Do you want anything to drink?

TERRY: Yes. I'd like some red wine, please.

WAITER: How much? A bottle?

TERRY: Er . . . I don't know. Do you want any wine, Janet?

JANET: No thanks. Not for me. But I'd like a glass of water.

TERRY: Oh, . . . and . . . I'd like a glass of red wine, please.

WAITER: Two pizzas with salami, a glass of red wine, and a glass of water. Is that all?

TERRY: Yes. That's all.

It is eight twenty now.

WAITER: Finished?

JANET: Yes. Thank you.

WAITER: Anything else?

TERRY: Do you want any coffee, Janet?

JANET: No. Look at the time, Terry. We've only got ten minutes.

TERRY: We'd like the bill, please.

WAITER: Yes, sir. It's coming.

JANET: Here's some money, Terry. I want to pay for my pizza.

TERRY: Oh. Thanks.

JANET: Come on, Terry. Let's pay and go.

2

1. What does Terry want?
2. What does Janet want?
3. What does Janet say about the wine?
4. What does Terry say to the waiter about the wine?
5. Terry asks Janet some questions. What are they?
6. Does Janet pay for her pizza? What does she say to Terry about this?

3

(a) *You are in a restaurant. Ask the waiter*

Have you got **any** ⎰ pizza with salami? / red wine? / Italian wine? / beer? / etc. ⎱

(b) *Now look at page 55. Ask the waiter more questions*

Have you got **any** ⎰ peas? / potatoes? / beans? / etc. ⎱

(c) *Now order things from the waiter. Look at page 55 again and say*

I'd / We'd ⎰ like **some** ____, please. ⎱

1

It is eleven o'clock in the evening and Janet is watching television. She can see pictures of New York. It is cold there and it is snowing. Can you see all that snow?

Janet is writing a letter, too.
Read the letter. Then ask people in your class questions about it

2

58 Albert Gardens
LONDON NW3
Monday Jan 16

Dear Dad,
    It is about eleven o'clock in the evening and I am sitting here in my flat watching the late news on television. I can see snow! And it is in New York.
    Thank God I am not in New York now! I don't like snow. I can't stand it! Do you remember?
    I like London. I am happy here. I think it is a wonderful city. There is only one thing I don't like. I can't stand the vegetables here. The meat is usually good but I think the vegetables are terrible. English people always boil them in a lot of water. They never have any taste.
    I've got a new boyfriend. His name is Terry Carter and he goes to London University. He is studying engineering. He wants to be an engineer.
    Well, that is all for now. I want a letter from you, too!
Love,
Janet

3

You are a friend of Janet's. You are phoning her from New York. It is six o'clock in the evening there.

JANET: Hello?
YOU: ___? Is ___ Janet?
JANET: Yes. ___ that?
YOU: This is ___
JANET: ___! Where ___ ___?
YOU: ___ in New York. How ___ ___?
JANET: Oh, ___ fine, but ___ ___ you?
YOU: ___, thanks. But ___ very cold here and ___ snowing.
JANET: I ___. I'm ___ television now and I ___ see all the ___
YOU: ___ ___ snowing ___, too?
JANET: No, ___ ___
YOU: ___ ___ like London?
JANET: Yes, ___ ___. And ___ ___ my flat here. Oh! ___ ___ a new boy friend.
YOU: ___ ___ name?
JANET: Terry. ___ a student, too.
YOU: ___ ___ go to the London School of Dance?
JANET: No, ___ ___. He ___ ___ London University.

Read this menu

Menu

Roast chicken, peas and roast or
boiled potatoes

Roast lamb, beans and roast or
boiled potatoes

Fried fillet of Sole, peas and chips
(fried potatoes)

Rump steak, peas and beans, chips
or boiled potatoes

Dessert

Vanilla or Chocolate Ice Cream

Fruit Salad with Cream

Cheese and Biscuits

2

Now order

WAITER: ___ I have your ___ now?
YOU: Yes. ___ ___ some ___, please.
WAITER: What ___ of vegetables ___ you want?
YOU: . . .
WAITER: ___ ___ want roast or boiled potatoes?
YOU: . . .
WAITER: Anything to drink? Wine? Beer?
YOU: . . .
WAITER: ___ that all?
YOU: . . .

And now you want to pay

YOU: . . .
WAITER: ___ coming.

3

*Read the letter from Janet to her father again. Then
ask and answer these questions*

1. ___ she ___ television now?
2. ___ ___ snowing in New York?
3. ___ ___ snowing in London, too?
4. ___ Janet like snow?
5. ___ ___ like London?
6. ___ ___ ___ the vegetables, too?
7. What ___ ___ want from ___ father?

4

This is a letter from Terry to his mother.

_____ Mum,
         _ _ about twelve o'clock
_ ___ evening. _ ___ sitting here ___ ___
bedsitter. ___ _____ to the radio, too
         _ ___ happy here in London
_ ____ it is a good city. And _ ____ a
new girlfriend. ___ _____ is Janet
Snow and ___ _ from New York.
         She __ _____ dancing at
the London School of Dance.
         _____ _ all for now.

         _____,
         Terry

1

It is Saturday morning, February 26th.
It is exactly seven thirty in the morning.
Mary works on Saturday. Peter doesn't.

PETER: Come on, Mary. Get up. It's seven thirty.

MARY: Oh, I don't want to get up this morning. And I don't want to work today. I want to sleep!

2

Simon Norris doesn't go to school on Saturday. It is eleven o'clock now and he and his father are in Regent's Park. There is a zoo in Regent's Park.

SIMON: Dad! I want to go to the zoo. I want to see the animals there!

PETER: All right. Let's go.

3

It is eleven thirty now. Terry Carter wants to go to "The Bell". But Janet wants to go to Regent's Park.

TERRY: Let's go to "The Bell". Let's have a drink there.

JANET: No! I don't want to go there now. Let's go to Regent's Park. Look! The sun's shining! Come on!

4

Do you remember Frank Mitchum? He is still in prison. He is standing at a window. Frank wants to leave the prison. He wants to walk in the streets. He wants to go to pubs, drink beer, sit in the sun and talk to women. But he can't.

a

PICTURE ONE

1. Where are Peter and Mary?
2. What does Mary do on Saturday?
3. What about Peter?
4. What is he saying to her?
5. And what is she saying to him?

PICTURE TWO

1. What time is it now?
2. Where are Simon and Peter?
3. What is Simon saying?
4. Does Peter want to go to the zoo, too?

PICTURE THREE

1. Where does Terry want to go?
2. What is he saying?
3. Does Janet want to go there?
4. Where does she want to go?
5. What is she saying?

PICTURE FOUR

1. *Talk about Frank Mitchum*
   He wants to . . .
2. *Ask and answer*
   Can Frank . . . ?
3. *What is Frank saying?*
   "I want to . . ."

b

1

Stop and Look

He She	wants	to go to ___
		to see ___
I We You They	want	to have a ___
		to sit in ___
		to eat ___
		to drink ___

2

Mary ___ to sleep. = *Mary wants to sleep.*

1. She doesn't want ___ ___ up.
2. Simon ___ ___ go to the zoo.
3. Peter ___ ___ ___ to the zoo, too.
4. They ___ ___ see the animals there.
5. Terry is saying: "I ___ ___ ___ a drink in 'The Bell'."
6. But Janet is saying: "I ___ ___ ___ to Regent's Park!"

3

Stop and Look

Let's { **go** to "The Bell".
have a drink there.
sit in the sun.
see the animals in the zoo. }

4

You are talking to a friend. You want to have a drink in "The Bell" with your friend. You can say:

Let's have a drink in "The Bell".

What can you say now? You want to

1. go to Regent's Park
2. go to a cinema
3. see a film
4. watch television
5. listen to the radio
6. have dinner in a restaurant
7. go there now

1 🔊

Terry and Janet often go to the cinema on Saturday.
They usually go in the evening. Here are six films.
They are on in London this week.

1

2

3

4

5

6

The six films are different. What kind are they?

One is a western.

Three is a love story.

Five is a disaster film.

Two is a war film.

Four is a horror film.

Six is a comedy.

What kind of films do you like?
Do you want to see a film this evening?
What kind?
What about science fiction films?
Do you like them, too?

d

1

Now listen to Terry and Janet

JANET: Let's go to the cinema this evening.
TERRY: All right. What do you want to see?
JANET: I don't know. What about you?
TERRY: Well, "The Last Bridge" is on at the Odeon here in Camden Town.
JANET: It's a war film, isn't it?
TERRY: That's right.
JANET: I don't like war films. I never go to them.
TERRY: Oh, well, here's a paper. You can see what's on at the other cinemas.
JANET: What about "A Star in the Night"?
TERRY: What kind of film is it?
JANET: It's a kind of . . . love story. But Barbara Streiser is in it. She sings, too. I think she's very good.
TERRY: I don't really like her. What else is on?
JANET: Hmm. Ahh! Here's a film for you. "Blood and the Vampire". I know you like *that* kind of film.
TERRY: A horror film? No. Not this evening.
JANET: What about a western?
TERRY: Is there a good one on?
JANET: What do you know about "The Sheriff"?
TERRY: Who's in it?
JANET: John Dane and Lauren Bacardi.
TERRY: Well, he's a good actor and she's a very good actress. Where's it on?
JANET: At the Classic. Do you want to see it?
TERRY: Yes. Good idea. When does it start?
JANET: At eight twenty.
TERRY: All right. Let's go.

2 Answer

1. What is "The Last Bridge"?
2. Does Janet want to see it?
3. Where is it on?
4. What is the Odeon?
5. Does Janet want to see "A Star in the Night"?
6. What does she say about it?
7. What does she say about Barbara Streiser?
8. And what does Terry say about her?
9. What kind of films does he like?
10. What does he want to see?
11. What about Janet?
12. Who's in the film and where is it on?

3

Now talk about the conversation

Janet wants to . . . this evening. They can see . . . It's on at . . . He/She wants to . . . He/She doesn't want to . . .

4

Mike Sutton and Anna Parker are talking.

MIKE: Let's ___ ___ the cinema.
ANNA: What ___ ___ ___ to see?
MIKE: "Blood and ___ ___"
ANNA: No, I don't ___ ___ films!
MIKE: Well what ___ "A Star ___ ___ ___"?
ANNA: ___ in it?
MIKE: Barbara ___
ANNA: And where's it ___?
MIKE: ___ the ABC.
ANNA: All right. ___ ___ see ___. When ___ ___ ___?
MIKE: At eight ten.

1

Laura works in the travel agency on Saturday. She is talking to a young married couple. Their names are Steve and Jenny.

JENNY: We'd like some information, please. We want to go to Los Angeles.
LAURA: Yes. What do you want to know?
JENNY: Well, first of all, we want to know the fare. The air fare, of course.
LAURA: When do you want to go?
STEVE: We don't really know. In July, or perhaps in June.
LAURA: I see. Well, in May and June the fare is £235. But it's less in March and April. It's only £220.
JENNY: And what about July?
LAURA: It's more in July.
STEVE: More? How much is it then?
LAURA: It's £262.
STEVE: Oh . . .
JENNY: Can you give us a brochure, please? We want to think about it.
LAURA: Yes, of course. Here you are.
STEVE: Thanks.
LAURA: That's all right.

2

Ask questions about Steve and Jenny. Give the answers, too

1. Where ___ they want ___ go?
2. ___ they ___ to ___ to Los Angeles in February?
3. ___ they ___ ___ go in March?
4. When ___ they ___ ___ go?

3

Now talk about the conversation

1. Steve and Jenny want ___ ___ ___ ___ ___
2. They ___ ___ go in ___ or perhaps in ___
3. The fare in ___ is ___
4. But in ___ the fare ___ ___

4

Now look at this information

Return Fares London-Los Angeles

01 Mar–30 Apr	£ 220
01 May–30 June	£ 235
01 July–31 July	£ 262
01 Aug–15 Sept	£ 285
16 Sept–15 Oct	£ 235
16 Oct–31 Dec	£ 220

1. What is the fare in April?
2. Is it the same in May?
3. Is it more or is it less in August?

Ask more questions

What is the fare in ___?
Is it more/the same/less in ___?

f

1

01 Aug–15 Sept	£ 285
16 Sept–15 Oct	£ 235
16 Oct–31 Dec	£ 220

Look at the fares for August, September, October, November and December again!

Before September 15th the fare is £285. But after September 15th the fare is £235.

And after October 15th it's only £220!

1. What is the fare before September 15th?
2. Is the fare the same after September 15th?
3. Is it more?
4. What can you say about the fare after October 15th?
5. You are going to Los Angeles after September 15th but before October 15th. How much do you pay?

2

Here is some more information from the brochure.
What does it tell you?

Return Fares London-Detroit

01 Apr–31 May	£ 152
01 Jun–13 July	£ 169
14 July–10 Sept	£ 199

Return Fares London-Toronto

01 Jun–13 July	£ 175
14 July–10 Sept	£ 189
11 Sept–08 Oct	£ 152

Talk about the fares

Before ___ the fare to ___ is £___
but **after** ___ the fare is £___

3

You and a friend are talking to Laura now.

YOU: ___ you give ___ some ___, please.
We ___ ___ ___ ___ Toronto.

LAURA: What ___ ___ ___ ___ know?

YOU: Well, ___ want ___ ___ to Toronto in September. ___ ___ ___ fare?

LAURA: Well, ___ September 10th, the ___ is £189 but ___ September 10th, it's £152.

YOU: Oh. ___ ___ give ___ a brochure?
We ___ ___ ___ ___ about it.

FOR EXTRA PRACTICE, SEE READ AND WRITE 3, PAGE 111

MARCH

Sun	Mon	Tues	Wed	Thur	Fri	Sat
=	=	1	2	3	4	5
6	7	8	9	10	11	12
13	14	15	16	17	18	19
20	21	22	23	24	25	26
27	28	29	30	(31)	=	=

Look at this calendar. It is March.
The date is Thursday, March 31st.
Yesterday was Wednesday, March 30th.
Last month was February, and the month
before that was January.

It is nine o'clock in the morning and Frank
Mitchum is in prison. But he is happy. He is
happy because today is his last day in prison.
The doors are opening.

GUARD: All right, Mitchum. You can leave
now.
FRANK: Goodbye.
GUARD: I don't want to see you again.
FRANK: And I don't want to see *you* again!

George King and Lucky Jones are outside the
prison. They are there because they want to talk
to Frank.

LUCKY: Look! There he is! He's coming now.
GEORGE: Good! But I don't want to talk to him
here. Follow him.

It is half past ten now and Frank is in Regent's
Park. He was in prison at nine. George and
Lucky were outside the prison.
But now Frank is free. That's why he is smiling.
He is smiling because he is free.
George and Lucky are in the park, too. Can
you see them?

a

PICTURE ONE

1. *Talk about the calendar you can see in the picture*

Today is ___, ___ ___
Yesterday was ___, ___ ___
Last month ___ ___

2. *Now talk about your calendar*

Today ___ ___, ___ ___
Yesterday ___ ___, ___ ___
Last month ___ ___

PICTURE TWO

1. What is the time?
2. Where is Frank?
3. Is he happy?
4. Why?

PICTURE THREE

Ask and answer

1. Where are . . . ?
2. Why are . . . ?
3. Is Frank . . . now?
4. Does George want . . . ?

PICTURE FOUR

1. Where is Frank now?
2. Where was he at nine?
3. Where are George and Lucky?
4. Where were they at nine?

b

1 **Stop and Look**

He She I It	was	in ___	yesterday. last month. last year. at ___ o'clock this morning.
You They We	were		

2 **Stop and Say**

It **is** ten o'clock. Frank **is** in Regent's Park.
He **was** in prison at nine. He **was** there yesterday, too.
George and Lucky **are** in Regent's Park now.
They **were** outside the prison at nine.

3

What about you?

1. Where were you yesterday?
2. Where were you last week?
3. And last month?
4. What about last year?

4 **Answer**

Yes, I was./No, I wasn't.
1. Were you in prison yesterday?
2. Were you in prison last year?
3. Were you in school yesterday?
4. Were you in school last week or last month?

5  **Ask people in your class ?** ...

Were you	in prison in England in a school in ___	**last year**? **last month**? **in 19 ___**?
Where **were** you		**in 19 ___**? **last year**? **at ___ o'clock yesterday**?

1

Frank is thinking. He doesn't know that George and Lucky are behind him.

"I'm free again! At nine o'clock this morning I was in prison but I'm out now! I don't want to go back there. I wasn't happy there. Things were terrible.

"But what can I do now? I can't go back to Manchester because my mother doesn't want to see me. And I don't want to stay in London because I haven't got a job. And I haven't got any money, either.

"Perhaps my father can help me. But where is he? Last year he was in Liverpool, I think. And the year before that he was in Leeds. But where is he now? I don't know.

"What about my sister? No! She can't help me because she's in Australia."

2

Ask questions about Frank.
What are the answers?

1. Is he ___ now?

2. Was he ___ { yesterday?
   last week?
   last month? }

3. Has he got ___ ___?
4. Can his father ___ ___?
   Can his sister ___ ___?
5. Does his mother want to ___ ___?
6. Does he want to ___ ___ ___?
7. Where was his father last ___?
   Where was his father ___ ___ ___ ___?

3

Now you are speaking to Frank.
Ask him questions

1. Are you ___ ___?
2. Were you ___ ___?
3. Have you got a ___?
   Have you got any ___?
4. Where is your ___?
5. Can he ___ ___?
   Can she ___ ___?
6. ___ your mother want to ___ ___?
7. Where was your father last ___?

4

1. Frank was . . .
2. He is . . .
3. He hasn't got . . .
4. His mother . . .
5. His father . . .
6. His sister . . .

5

What about you?

| Have you got a | brother? |
| | sister? |

| Where **was** | he | last year? |
| | she | last month? |

1

George and Lucky want to talk to Frank. But why?
Listen

LUCKY: Hello, Frankie. How are you?

FRANK: Lucky! What are you doing here? George! You're here, too. But . . .

LUCKY: We were outside the prison this morning. At nine o'clock.

FRANK: Were you? But I didn't see you.

GEORGE: No. But we saw you. And we followed you. We want to talk to you, Frank.

FRANK: Why? What do you want?

LUCKY: Let's go to George's house.

FRANK: Go to George's house? Why?

GEORGE: Because we want to talk to you!

LUCKY: We've got a job for you, Frank.

GEORGE: And there's money in it.

FRANK: A job? Money? What are you talking about? Look! Why are you here? Come on! Tell me!

GEORGE: We can't! Not here.

LUCKY: That's why we want to go to George's house. We want to talk about the job.

FRANK: Look! I . . . I don't want to talk to you about a job! No more jobs for me! Not with you.

LUCKY: Not with us? Why?

FRANK: Because I don't want to go back to prison again! That's why.

GEORGE: Don't you want to know more about the job?

FRANK: No! I don't want to know anything about the job! I'm leaving! Goodbye!

LUCKY: Frankie boy! Stop! Talk to us. Listen!

GEORGE: That's all right, Lucky. He doesn't want to talk to us now. But wait! That's all. Wait!

2 Answer

1. Does Frank know Lucky?
2. Does he know George, too?
3. Does he want to talk to them?
4. What do they want to do?
5. Why do they want to talk to him?
6. What does George say about the job?
7. Does Frank want to know about the job?
8. Does he want to work with George and Lucky?
9. Why doesn't he want to work with them?

3

You are Frank. Lucky says:

> We want to talk to you.

You say:

> **Why do you want to talk to me?**

Ask more questions with "Why . . . ?"
Lucky says

1. We want to see you.
2. We want to go to George's house.
3. We want to tell you about an American girl.
4. We watch her.
5. We follow her.
6. We are going to her flat now.

4 Speak and Write

1. At nine o'clock Lucky and George ___ ___ ___ ___
2. They saw ___ but Frank didn't ___ ___
3. They ___ him to Regent's Park.
4. Now they want to ___ ___ ___
5. But Frank doesn't want ___ ___ ___ ___
6. He doesn't want to ___ ___ ___ because . . .

1

Let's learn more about Frank.

Frank was born in Manchester. His mother was a waitress and his father was a bus driver. They were born in Manchester, too.

Frank started school when he was five. He was in school for eleven years. He wasn't very happy at school. And he wasn't very good at school, either.

He left school when he was sixteen.

His first job was in a supermarket. He was there for two years. His next job was in a factory.
He came to London when he was eighteen. He worked in a supermarket in London, too.
He went to prison last year. He is twenty years old now. He was in prison for three months but he is free now.

2 *What is Frank saying?*
1. I ___ born ___ ___
2. My parents ___ born ___ ___, ___
3. My mother ___ ___ ___ and my father ___ ___ ___
4. I started school when ___ ___ ___
5. I ___ very happy at school.
6. I left school when ___ ___ ___
   etc.

3 *What about you?*
1. I ___ born in ___
2. My parents ___ born ___ ___
3. I started ___ when I ___ ___
4. I left ___ when I ___ ___
5. My first job ___ in a ___

f

1

Was Frank born in Manchester?	→	Yes, he **was**.
Was Janet born there?	→	No, she **wasn't**.
Were Frank's parents born there?	→	Yes, they **were**.
Were Janet's parents born there?	→	No, they **weren't**.

Where **were** you born? → I **was** born in ___

Where **were** your parents born? → They **were** born in ___

2

1. Where ___ Frank born?
   He ___ ___ in Manchester.

2. ___ his parents born there, too?
   Yes, ___ ___

3. ___ Frank happy at school?
   No, ___ ___

4. ___ ___ very good at school?
   ___ , ___ ___

5. ___ ___ his first job?
   ___ a supermarket.

6. And ___ ___ ___ next job?
   ___ a factory.

7. Where ___ the factory?
   ___ ___

8. How old ___ he when he ___ to London?
   ___ ___ ___

3

You are asking Frank questions

1. YOU : ___ ___ ___ ___
   FRANK : Me? In Manchester.

2. YOU : ___ ___ ___ ___ ___, too?
   FRANK : Yes, they were.

3. YOU : ___ ___ ___ ___ ___?
   FRANK : At school? Well, I wasn't very good and I wasn't very bad, either.

4. YOU : ___ ___ ___ first job?
   FRANK : My first job? In a supermarket in Manchester.

5. YOU : How old ___ ___ when you ___ to London?
   FRANK : I was 18. I'm 20 now. But tell me something now! Why are you asking all these questions?

1

This is Laura Francis again. Do you remember her? Laura works in a travel agency now.
She likes her job. She lives in Watford with her father.
She starts work at nine and finishes at five thirty.
Laura is happy in her job now. Mary Norris is her boss.

2

But things were different last year. Last year she worked in an office. She typed letters all day.
Her boss was a man called Mr Carson.
She started at half past eight and finished at five.
Laura lived in Watford last year, too.

3

Mary Norris works in a travel agency and Peter Norris works in a factory in London now.
Things were the same last year.
But what about before that?

4

Before they came to London, Peter and Mary lived in Swindon. They worked there too.
Swindon is a town between London and Bristol.
Peter worked in a big factory there.
Mary worked in a small travel agency in Swindon. She managed the agency. She manages the agency in Camden Town, too.

a

PICTURE ONE

Ask and answer

1. Where . . .
2. ___ ___ like ___ ___?
3. Does ___ ___ with her father?
4. When ___ ___ start work?
5. ___ ___ ___ finish ___?
6. ___ ___ happy?

PICTURE TWO

Now speak about last year

1. Last year Laura ___ ___ an office.
2. ___ ___ letters.
3. Her boss ___ ___ ___ ___ ___
4. She ___ ___ Watford.

PICTURE THREE

What questions can you ask about Mary and Peter this year?

PICTURE FOUR

Can you ask questions about Peter and Mary before they came to London?

Did	Peter Mary	work in ___? live in ___?

Yes,	he she	**did.**
No,	he she	**didn't.**

→

b

1 *Stop and Look*

LAURA: I **live** in Watford now. I **lived** there last year, too. But last year I **worked** in an office and now I **work** in a travel agency.

2 **What about you?**

Where did you live last year?
Where do you live now?
Have you got a job now? Where do you work?
Did you work last year? Where?

Speak and Write

I **live** in ___ now and last year I **lived** in ___
I **worked** in ___ last year and now I **work** in ___

I haven't got a job now but last year/in 19___/last month/
etc. I worked in ___

3 **Ask people in your class**

Where **did** you	**live** **work**	in 19 ___? last year? last November?

→	Last ___ In 19___	I	**worked** **lived**	in ___

1 Laura is talking about her old job and her new job. *Listen*

LAURA: Last year I worked in an office in Watford. That was before I got a job in a travel agency in Camden Town.

We started every morning at half past eight and we finished at five. We had an hour for lunch.

The pay wasn't very good. I earned only £35 a week. And I wasn't very happy there.

My boss was a man called Mr Carson. He was nice and I liked him. But the work wasn't interesting. I mean, I typed letters all day and answered the phone.

One day I bought a newspaper and saw an advertisement. A travel agency in Camden Town wanted a young person with two foreign languages. Well, I can speak French, German and Italian. I went to the travel agency and saw Mary Norris. She asked me some questions and then she gave me the job.

I earn more in my new job. I think it's very interesting. I'm happy here.

1. Last year Laura ___ in an office but now she ___ in a travel agency.
2. Laura ___ happy in her old job but now she ___ very happy.
3. In her old job, she ___ letters all day and ___ the phone.
4. She ___ every morning at half past eight and ___ at five.
5. She ___ an hour for lunch in her old job.
6. One day she ___ a newspaper and ___ an advertisement.
7. She ___ to the travel agency and ___ Mary Norris.
8. Mary ___ her a lot of questions and Laura ___ them.
9. Mary ___ her the job.
10. In her old job Laura ___ £35 a week.
11. She ___ more now. Her pay ___ £40 a week.
12. She ___ at nine now and ___ at half past five. And she ___ an hour for lunch.

2

PRESENT (now)		PAST (yesterday, last week, etc.)	
He She	I We You They	He She I We You They	
↓	↓	↓	
works lives starts finishes types answers wants likes earns	work live start finish type answer want like earn	work ed live d start ed finish ed type d answer ed want ed like d earn ed	These are called *regular verbs*

He She	I We You They	He She I We You They	
↓	↓	↓	
goes comes leaves buys gives thinks sees has gets	go come leave buy give think see have get	went came left bought gave thought saw had got	And these are called *irregular verbs*

e

1

It is Wednesday, April 13th now. Frank came out of prison last month. He is having an interview for a job.

Listen

MAN: Do you mind if I ask you some questions?
FRANK: No, that's all right.
MAN: Where did you go to school, Frank?
FRANK: In Manchester. I was born there.
MAN: When did you leave school?
FRANK: When I was sixteen.
MAN: Which subjects did you study?
FRANK: Which subjects?
MAN: Yes. Did you study maths? Any foreign languages? What?
FRANK: Well . . . er . . . I studied maths . . . yeah . . . and . . . er . . . French and, uhm . . . history. You know . . . the usual things.
MAN: Which subjects did you like?
FRANK: Like? Oh . . . uh . . . English. I liked English. But I didn't like maths.
MAN: And French? Did you like French?
FRANK: Well, it was . . . all right. You know.
MAN: Were you good at it?
FRANK: Well, you know, I was . . . all right. Not good. Not bad. It wasn't very interesting.
MAN: Hmm. And when did you come to London?
FRANK: When I was eighteen.
MAN: Where did you work?
FRANK: In a supermarket. I . . . er . . . I finished in December. Last year.
MAN: Oh? Why did you leave the job? And what did you do then?
FRANK: Well, I finished because . . . because . . . I went to prison.
MAN: What? You went to prison?
FRANK: Yeah. I came out last month.
MAN: Oh? Hmm. I see. I see.

2

1. He ___ school ___ ___ ___ sixteen.
2. He studied ___, ___, and ___
3. He liked ___
4. He didn't like ___
5. ___ ___ to London when he was eighteen.
6. He ___ in a supermarket.
7. ___ ___ in December.
8. He ___ to prison in December and ___ ___ out last month.

3

What about you?

Where did you go to school?
Which subjects did you study?
Which subjects did you like?

Were you good at
$\begin{cases} \text{maths?} \\ \text{history?} \\ \text{English?} \\ \text{foreign languages?} \end{cases}$

When did you leave school?

4

Did you study ___?
Were you good at ___?
When did you leave school?
etc.

f

1

Stop and Look

Frank [worked] in a supermarket.
Janet [came] to England.
I [went] to ___
You [bought] a___
We [saw] ___
Peter and Mary [wanted] ___

[Did]	he [work] in a supermarket?		→	Yes,	he she I	**did**.
	she [come] to England?					
	I [go] ___ ?					
	you [buy] ___ ?		No,	we you they	**didn't**.
	we [see] ___?					
	they [want] ___ ?					

2

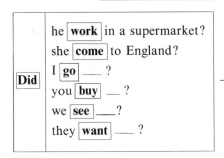

Read this about Anna Parker

Anna got up at seven o'clock yesterday.

She went to work at nine. She walked there.

She had lunch at one o'clock.

She finished work at five thirty.

In the evening she watched television and listened to the radio.

Mike Sutton went to the cinema last night and saw a film.

3

 Speak and Write

1. When ___ Anna ___ up yesterday?
   She ___ up at seven.

2. ___ she ___ to work at eight?
   No, ___ ___

3. When ___ she ___ to work?
   She ___ to work at nine.

4. ___ she ___ lunch at twelve?
   No, she ___ lunch at one.

5. ___ she ___ to the cinema yesterday evening?
   No, ___ ___

6. ___ Mike ___ to the cinema?
   Yes, ___ ___

4

  Ask people in your class

1. When ___ ___ ___ up?
2. When ___ ___ ___ to work/school?
3. ___ you ___ lunch at one o'clock, too?
4. ___ you ___ television in the evening?
5. ___ you ___ to the radio?

5

 What about you?

1. I ___ up at ___
2. I ___ to work/school at ___
3. I ___ lunch at ___
4. In the evening I . . .

1

Look at the date again. It is Thursday, April 14th now.
What did Frank Mitchum do yesterday?

2

He got up at seven and washed and shaved. Then he had breakfast. After that he went out and bought a newspaper.

3

He saw an advertisement in it. The advertisement said: "Wanted: Young people to work in radio factory". There were a lot of advertisements in the paper. But Frank wanted to know more about the job in the radio factory.

4

Frank went to the factory. He sat down in a big room and waited. There were a lot of other people in the room, too. They all wanted to work in the factory.

5

Then a man came into the room and said "Follow me, please." They went to an office and sat down. The man asked Frank a lot of questions. Frank answered them.

6

Frank wasn't happy when he came out of the factory. The man didn't give Frank a job because Frank came out of prison last month. He can't find a job because he was in prison. Frank is very unhappy today. He was unhappy yesterday, too.

a

These things are wrong.

It was Tuesday yesterday.

= **No! It was Wednesday yesterday.**

1. Frank got up at eight yesterday.
2. Then he had lunch.
3. He went out and bought a magazine.
4. Frank went to a supermarket.
5. The job was in a cinema.
6. He sat down in a small room.
7. They all wanted to buy food in the factory.
8. A woman interviewed Frank.
9. Frank asked a lot of questions.
10. The man answered them.
11. Frank was happy when he came out.
12. The man gave Frank the job.
13. Frank came out of prison yesterday.

b

1

Frank is telling you what he did yesterday.

1. ___ ___ ___ at seven.
2. Then I ___ and ___
3. After that I ___ ___
4. Then ___ ___ ___ ___ ___ a newspaper.
   etc.

2

You are asking Frank questions about yesterday

YOU: ___ ___ ___ ___ ___ ___?

FRANK: At seven.

YOU: ___ ___ ___ ___ ___?

FRANK: Yes, of course I washed and shaved yesterday! What a question! And after that I went out and bought a newspaper.

YOU: Why ___ ___ ___ ___ ___?

FRANK: Because I wanted to find a job.

Now go on. Can you ask more questions about yesterday? What are the answers?

3

Ask people in your class about yesterday

When **did** you	**get up**?
	have breakfast?
	go to work/school?
	come home?

What **did** you **do**	**before**	breakfast?
		you went to ___?
	after	you came home?
		dinner?

MONDAY 4 APRIL	*Go to Manchester, train leaves 8·52. Arrive Manchester 11·30.*
TUESDAY 5 APRIL	*See manager of new factory, have lunch with him.*
WEDNESDAY 6 APRIL	*Come back to London (train 8·32 — London 10·42).*
THURSDAY 7 APRIL	*Buy new machines for factory.*
FRIDAY 8 APRIL	*Find new secretary!*
SATURDAY 9 APRIL	*Go to zoo with Simon.*
SUNDAY 10 APRIL	*Have lunch with Mary's mother.*

1

This is a page from Peter Norris's diary. He did these things **last week**.

2 *What did Peter do last week?*

He ___ ___ ___ on Monday. The train ___ at ___ and ___ in Manchester at ___ On Tuesday he . . . etc.

Now ask questions

Did he . . . on Monday?
When did . . . ?
What did . . . on ___ ?

3

These two tickets were in Anna Parker's handbag. As you can see, they are old tickets.

Queen Elizabeth Hall
LONDON CONCERT ORCHESTRA

FRIDAY, 11 February, 7.45 pm

Rear Stalls £1.50	Row **GG**	Seat **33**

(a) *Ask and answer questions about the concert ticket*

When ___ the concert?
When did Anna ___ to the concert?
Where ___ she sit?
How much ___ she pay for the ticket?
When ___ the concert start?

0678
2nd-Return

LONDON
to
BRIGHTON

Fare
£5·90

Valid
3 months
15 April

(b) *Ask questions about the rail ticket*

Where . . . ?
When . . . ?
How much . . . ?

d

1 ⊚

Mike Sutton is telling his class a story. It is a story about himself and Anna Parker.
Listen

Yesterday evening I met my girlfriend at eight o'clock and we went to the cinema. We saw a western. Charles Bronson was in it. We liked it.

After the cinema we went to an Indian restaurant and had some curry. Then we walked home. My girlfriend . . . her name is Anna . . . and I had a cup of coffee in her flat. We talked about the film. I left her flat about midnight and walked home.

But when I got home my keys weren't in my pocket. Well, what did I do? I climbed through a window. But one of my neighbours saw me. She thought I was a burglar. You see, there was a burglar in my flat last December. She phoned the police. I was in bed when they came.

I found my keys this morning. They were in the pocket of another jacket.

2

Yesterday evening Mike . . .

3

You are speaking to Mike. Ask him questions about yesterday evening

What . . . ?
What kind . . . ?
Why . . . ? Did . . . ?
Where . . . ?
When . . . ?

1

These are *regular verbs*.

walk	I **walked** to my friend's flat last night.
watch	We **watched** a film on TV.
start	It **started** at 9 o'clock.
finish	It **finished** at 10.30.
like	I **liked** it very much.
phone	Later I **phoned** my mother.
talk	We **talked** about the film.

And these are *irregular verbs*.

go	My friend and I **went** to the cinema last night.
meet	We **met** outside the cinema.
see	We **saw** an old western.
leave	We **left** the cinema about ten.
eat	We **ate** some spaghetti in an Italian restaurant.
drink	We **drank** some wine, too.
have	Then we **had** some coffee.
get	I **got** home about midnight.
find	I **found** a letter there for me.
sit/read	I **sat** down and **read** it.

2

Laura usually (go) to work on the train. She (go) to work on the train yesterday, too. It (come) at half past eight. She (get on) it, and (sit down). She (see) a friend on the train. They (talk) about work and things like that. She (get off) at Camden Town Station and (walk) to the travel agency. Then she (start) work. She (finish) at half past five yesterday. At six she (meet) some friends near Oxford Circus. They (have) dinner in a small Italian restaurant.

3

What about you?

1. When do you usually get up?
2. What do you usually have for breakfast?
3. When do you usually leave for school or work?
4. Where do you usually have lunch?
5. When do you usually go home?
6. What do you usually do in the evening? (watch TV? meet some friends?)

4

Now Laura is telling you what she did

I usually ___ ___ ___ on the ___. Yesterday I ___ ___ ___ on the ___, too. When it ___, I g___ on it and ___ down. I ___ a friend ___ ___ ___. We ___ about ___ ___ ___ ___ ___. I ___ off at Camden Town Station and ___ to the travel agency. Then I ___ ___. I ___ at half past five and at six I ___ two friends near Oxford Circus. We ___ dinner in ___ ___ ___ ___.

5

What about you?

What did you do yesterday?

I ___ up at ___
I ___ ___ for breakfast.
I ___ to school/work at ___ ___
I started/finished at ___ ___
Then I . . .

f

1

What about Frank? He can't find a job and he is very unhappy. He is sitting in the park again.

Someone wants to talk to him there. Who?

LUCKY: Hello, Frankie boy. Do you mind if I sit down?

FRANK: Oh, it's you again, Lucky.

LUCKY: I saw you yesterday, Frankie. I followed you to that factory.

FRANK: What? You followed me? Why?

LUCKY: Because we're very interested in you, Frankie. Well, did you find a job yesterday? Did they give you a job yesterday?

FRANK: I think you know the answer.

LUCKY: Yeah, of course I do. Well . . . you can work for us, you know.

FRANK: Look! Do you mind if I ask you something?

LUCKY: No, that's all right. Go ahead, kid.

FRANK: You always talk about a job. But what is it?

LUCKY: I can't tell you that. But I can tell you this. There's a lot of money in it. I told you that before, when I saw you here. Do you want to know more? Are you interested?

FRANK: I . . . I . . .

LUCKY: Because if you want to know more, I mean if you're really interested, George can tell you more. Are you coming?

FRANK: I . . . yes! Come on! Let's go.

2

1. What did Lucky do yesterday?
2. And what did Frank do?
3. What are they doing now?
4. Where are they going?
5. Why are they going there?

3

Do you mind if I . . .?

Frank wants to sit down. He says:

Do you mind if I sit down?

What do you say? You want to

1. open the window
2. have a sandwich now
3. smoke
4. leave the class before the lesson finishes
5. shut the door
6. ask some questions

4

What do you think?

What is this "job"? Perhaps this information can help you.

George King wants more money. He knows there is a rich American girl in London. He knows her father is the president of a bank. Who is this girl? Why is George interested in her? What does he want to do?

FOR EXTRA PRACTICE, SEE READ AND WRITE 4, PAGE 113

1

It is Friday evening, May 20th. Terry is waiting for Janet in front of a cinema. The film is starting now but Janet isn't there. Terry is thinking.

TERRY : I don't understand it. Janet never comes late. Why isn't she here? What's the matter?

2

It is almost midnight now. Terry is phoning Janet. Terry saw the film. He didn't see all of it. It started at 8.30. He waited for fifteen minutes. Then he went in. Janet didn't see the film. She didn't come to the cinema.

TERRY : No answer! Where is she? Why didn't she come to the cinema? What's the matter with her?

3

It is Saturday morning now. Terry is phoning again. He phoned last night but Janet didn't answer then. And she isn't answering now.

TERRY : No answer again! And she didn't answer last night. Where can she be? I'm worried! I'm very worried!

4

This is Janet's bed. She didn't sleep in it last night. She didn't go to the cinema last night. She wasn't in her flat. She didn't come home.

She ran in Regent's Park yesterday morning. But she didn't come back. She didn't have breakfast. She didn't listen to the radio. She didn't go to the London School of Dance.

a

PICTURE ONE

Ask and answer

1. Where is ___?
2. Is the film ___?
3. Is Janet ___?
4. Does she often ___ ___?

PICTURE TWO

1. What is Terry doing now?
2. Why?
3. Is Janet answering?
4. *Ask and answer*
   Did Janet . . . ?
   Did Terry . . . ?

PICTURE THREE

1. What did Terry do last night?
2. What is he doing now?
3. He is worried. Why?
4. What is he saying?

PICTURE FOUR

Ask and answer

1. Did Janet ___ yesterday?
2. Was she in her ___?
3. ___ ___ ___ in Regent's Park?
4. ___ ___ ___ to the radio?
   etc.

b

1 **Stop and Look**

He She I You We They	didn't	**go** to the cinema **answer** the phone **see** a film **have** breakfast **run** in Regent's Park	yesterday. last week. at ___ o'clock.

2 Speak and Write

(a) Terry did these things yesterday. But Janet didn't.

EXAMPLE: Terry went to the cinema.
= **Janet didn't go to the cinema**.

1. He came at eight thirty.
2. He waited.
3. He went into the cinema.
4. He went to a pub after the film.
5. He saw Mike Sutton.
6. He talked to him.
7. He had a drink.
8. He went home.
9. He slept in a bed last night.

(b) *Ask questions about Janet*
Why didn't she . . . ?

EXAMPLE: Terry went to the cinema (but Janet didn't).
= **Why didn't she go to the cinema?**

1. Terry came on time.
2. He saw the film.
3. He went home.
4. He slept in a bed.
5. He got up the next morning.
6. He had breakfast.
7. He had a shower, too.

What about you?

(c) *Did you do these things yesterday?*

EXAMPLE: see a film
= **I saw a film yesterday.**
or **I didn't see a film yesterday.**

1. go to work
2. go to school
3. smoke ten cigars
4. have dinner in a restaurant
5. watch television
6. see a film
7. have a drink in a pub
8. sleep in a bed
9. sleep in prison

84

C

It is Saturday afternoon. Terry is phoning Anna Parker. *Listen*

TERRY: Hello, Anna. This is Terry.

ANNA: Oh, hello, Terry. How are things?

TERRY: Well, I'm all right, but I'm worried about Janet.

ANNA: Worried about Janet? Why? What's the matter with her?

TERRY: I don't know.

ANNA: I'm sorry, Terry. I don't understand. What . . . what do you mean?

TERRY: Well, you see, we had a date last night. I mean, we wanted to see a film. But she didn't come.

ANNA: Yes? And did you phone her?

TERRY: Yes, I did. But she didn't answer. I phoned last night. And I phoned this morning again.

ANNA: Oh, well, perhaps she . . .

TERRY: Listen, please. So after I phoned this morning, I went to her flat. I knocked on the door. She didn't answer then, either. I mean, she didn't come to the door. She wasn't in the flat. I'm sure.

ANNA: Did you ask her neighbours about her? You know, those people in the flat above her. What's their name? Norris, I think.

TERRY: Yes, I did. I talked to a young boy . . . Simon, I think his name is. He saw her yesterday morning. She ran in Regent's Park but he says she didn't come back. I mean, he didn't see her.

ANNA: Really? Hmm. That's strange.

TERRY: Yes, it is. It's very strange. I . . . I can't understand it.

2

1. Why is Terry phoning Anna?
2. What did he and Janet want to do yesterday evening?
3. When did Terry phone Janet?
4. Why is he worried about her now?
5. What did he do after he phoned her this morning?
6. Who did Terry talk to?
7. What did Simon tell Terry?

3

1. When ___ Terry and Janet have a date?
2. ___ Anna worried about Janet, too?
3. ___ Janet in her flat yesterday evening?
4. ___ Terry phone her yesterday?
5. ___ he go to her flat this morning?
6. ___ she there?
7. ___ she answer the door?

4

Terry talked to Simon Norris this morning. *What were his questions?*

TERRY: . . . ?

SIMON: Yes, I know her. I often see her.

TERRY: . . . ?

SIMON: Yesterday? Yes, I saw her yesterday.

TERRY: . . . ?

SIMON: When? Well . . . er . . . in the morning. She went out at seven. She ran in the park.

TERRY: . . . ?

SIMON: When? Well, that's strange but she didn't come back. I mean, I didn't see her. And I can always see her from my window.

d

1

This building was a factory. But it isn't a factory now. People don't work here any more.

It is in Camden Town, very near a canal. The canal is behind the building. Can you see it?

There are four people in the old factory. One of the four is Janet Snow.

Janet can't see the building. She doesn't know where she is. She can't see anything. There is a blindfold over her eyes.

She can't move her arms or legs. There are ropes around them. Janet is tied to a chair. She can't stand up. She can't sleep. She can't talk.

But what happened yesterday? Why is Janet in the old factory now?

Janet left her flat at seven. She ran in the park. Lucky Jones and Frank Mitchum were there. They watched her. She didn't see them. When Janet came back, they stopped her. Lucky had a gun. He and Frank had a van, too.

"Don't shout. Don't talk. Don't run. Get into the van!" they told her.

Janet got into the van. That's why she isn't in her flat now. Lucky and Frank kidnapped her yesterday.

2

Where is . . . ? **Can** Janet . . . ? **When did** . . . ?
Did Janet . . . ? **When did** Lucky and Frank . . . ?

e

1

This man is worried about Janet, too. He is Janet's father and his name is Mr Howard Snow. He works in a bank. But he isn't a clerk. He is the president. Mr Snow is a very rich man.

Mr Snow always works six days a week. He works on Saturday, too. On Saturday he usually gets up at seven thirty. Then he has breakfast. After that he reads the paper. And after that he goes to work. He usually works four hours on Saturday. He starts at nine and finishes at one. He often plays golf in the afternoon. Sometimes he plays tennis. But he didn't do any of these things this morning or this afternoon. George King phoned him early this morning. And now Mr Snow is at Kennedy Airport in New York. He is waiting for a plane to London.

It is 10 pm, Saturday evening, May 21st.

2

Who . . . ?   Where . . . ?   When does he usually . . . ?

Does he usually . . . on Saturday?   Did he . . . $\begin{cases} \textbf{this morning?} \\ \textbf{this afternoon?} \end{cases}$

3

(a) Remember! It is Saturday evening now.

What are the things Mr Snow usually does in the morning and in the afternoon?

Talk about them

He usually . . . but this $\begin{cases} \textbf{morning} \\ \textbf{afternoon} \end{cases}$ he didn't . . .

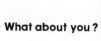**What about you?**

(b)

What do you usually do every day? Did you do these things last Saturday too?

EXAMPLE: **I usually go to school/work every day but I didn't go to school/work last Saturday.**

(c) Janet often does these things on Friday. She didn't do them yesterday.

EXAMPLE: She has breakfast.
        = **She didn't have breakfast yesterday.**

1. She listens to the radio.
2. She leaves the flat after breakfast.
3. She goes to school.
4. She sees her friends.
5. She dances.
6. She goes to "The Bell".
7. She writes her father a letter.

She didn't do other things yesterday. What were they?

f

1

And this is what George said to Mr Snow at seven o'clock this morning (New York time). *Listen*

MR SNOW: H . . . hello?

GEORGE: Is that Mr Howard Snow?

MR SNOW: Yes. Who's that? What time is it? You woke me up!

GEORGE: Listen to me, Mr Snow. I'm phoning from London. And I'm phoning about your daughter.

MR SNOW: My daughter? Janet? What's the matter? Is she . . .?

GEORGE: She's all right. We've got her, Mr Snow. Do you understand? We've got her.

MR SNOW: You've got her? What do you mean? What do you want to tell me? What is this? A joke?

GEORGE: A joke? No, Mr Snow, it isn't a joke. I'm not laughing.

MR SNOW: I don't understand.

GEORGE: Do you understand this? We kidnapped her yesterday. And now we want a million dollars for her.

MR SNOW: What? You . . . you what?

GEORGE: Yes, I think you understand now. There's a plane from New York to London at eleven o'clock this evening. Get on that plane, Mr Snow. Get on it!

MR SNOW: And then? What then?

GEORGE: There's a hotel in London called "The Park Hotel". I think you know it. Stay there. And wait.

MR SNOW: Wait? Wait for what?

GEORGE: My next phone call. At nine o'clock tomorrow evening. At "The Park Hotel". That's all now.

MR SNOW: Wait! Stop! Who are you? What's your name? Hello? Hello?

2

1. Where do you think Mr Snow was when George phoned?
2. Does Mr Snow know George?
3. Does Mr Snow think this is a joke?
4. What does George want?

3 (Stop and Look)

New York Time

It is twelve o'clock noon in New York now. It is Saturday. George phoned Mr Snow at seven.

He **is going to** phone him tomorrow, too.

He **is going to** phone him at nine o'clock.

Mr Snow is in New York now.

He **is going to** be in London on Sunday.

4

Now speak and write about George and Mr Snow

1. George ___ going ___ phone Mr Snow tomorrow.
2. George ___ ___ to phone ___ at nine o'clock.
3. Mr Snow ___ ___ ___ be in London tomorrow.

5 (Answer)

1. Is Mr Snow going to get on a plane?
2. Which plane is he going to get on?
3. Is he going to stay in a hotel in London?
4. Which hotel is he going to stay at?
5. What is he going to do at the hotel?
6. George wants a million dollars from him. Is he going to give George the million dollars? What do you think?

I **think** }
I **don't think** } he **is going to give** . . .

11 PM, SATURDAY EVENING
KENNEDY AIRPORT, NEW YORK
A plane is taking off. It is flying to London and
Mr Snow is on it.
You can see another plane, too.
It isn't taking off. It is going to take off.
It is going to take off in a minute.

ON THE PLANE

Mr Snow is going to smoke a cigarette.
But first he wants to know something.

MR SNOW: When are we going to arrive in
        London?
STEWARDESS: In five hours, sir.
MR SNOW: I mean, what time are we going to
        arrive there? London time.
STEWARDESS: Nine o'clock, sir.

LONDON 5 O'CLOCK, SUNDAY MORNING

The sun is shining. It is early in the morning. It
is going to be a warm day.
But look at those clouds.
Perhaps it is going to rain.

IN THE FACTORY

Janet can't sleep. Frank is sleeping in a chair
near her. She is thinking.

JANET: What are they going to do to me? Am I
      going to see Terry, my father and my
      friends again? Or are they going to kill
      me?
      What am I going to do?

a

PICTURE ONE

1. Look at the two planes. What can you say about one of them?
2. What can you say about the other one?
3. What questions can you ask about Mr Snow?
   Is . . . ?
   Where . . . ?

PICTURE TWO

1. Is Mr Snow smoking a cigarette?
2. Is he going to smoke it?
3. What time is he going to arrive in London?
4. What is his question?

PICTURE THREE

1. What is the time in London?
2. Do you think it is going to rain?
3. Is it raining now?
4. What kind of day do you think it is going to be?

PICTURE FOUR

1. What can you say about Janet and Frank?
2. *Ask questions about her*
   Are they going to . . . ?
   Is she going to . . . ?
3. What are some of the answers? What do you think?

b

1 **Stop and Say**

It is twelve o'clock midnight.
Mr Snow **is sitting** in a plane.
He **is flying** to London.
He **is thinking** about Janet.
He **is going to arrive** in London at nine o'clock (London time).
He **is going to arrive** there in four hours.
He **is going to stay** at "The Park Hotel".
George **is going to phone** him at
nine o'clock in the evening.

2

Mr Snow is speaking now. What is he saying?

> **I'm ___ing now.**
> **I'm going to . . .**

3

Janet usually does these things on Sunday.
Is she going to do them today?
Is she going to . . . ?

   No, she isn't.
→ No, I don't think she is.
   No, I'm sure she isn't.

1. She runs in Regent's Park.
2. She has a shower and a big breakfast.
3. She listens to the radio.
4. She reads the newspapers.
5. She has lunch with Terry.
6. She goes for a walk.
7. She sees her friends.

1 It is eight forty five now. Mary and Peter Norris are still in bed. They usually get up at nine on Sunday.

Are they getting up now? Or are they going to get up?

Here are some other things they usually do on Sunday.

1. They have breakfast at nine thirty.
2. They read the Sunday papers.
3. They walk in the park before lunch.
4. They have tea with Mary's mother. She lives in another part of London.
5. Sometimes Peter plays golf in the afternoon.
6. After dinner they watch television or listen to the radio.

Look at the pictures (1–6). Are they doing these things? Or are they going to do them?

2

Look at the pictures again

Is Are	—	going to (do)?	or	Is Are	—	—ing?

EXAMPLE:

PICTURE ONE: Are they having breakfast? – No, they aren't.
Are they going to have breakfast? – Yes, they are.

3

What about you?

What do you usually do on Sunday? → **I usually . . .**
What about next Sunday? **Next Sunday I think I'm going to . . .**

d

1

	MAY		JUNE	
Sun	(22)	29		5
Mon	23	20		6
Tues	24	31		7
Wed	25		1	8
Thurs	26		2	9
Fri	27		3	10
Sat	28		4	11

Look at the calendar

Today is Sunday, May 22nd.
Tomorrow is Monday, May 23rd.
The day after tomorrow is Tuesday.

Next week starts on Sunday, May 29th.
Next month is June.

We can't see the year. What year is it now?
What about next year?

This is the calendar in the book.
But what about your calendar?

Look at it. Then answer these questions

1. What is today?
2. What is tomorrow?
3. And the day after tomorrow?

4. When does next week start?
5. Which month is next month?
6. Talk about this year and next year:
   This year is 19 ___
   Next year is 19 ___

2

Janet is in a factory in Camden Town today.
Is she going to be there tomorrow, too? She doesn't know.
She is thinking.

JANET: Where am I now? What kind of place is this? I think it's
a factory, but I'm not sure. Yes! It's probably a
factory. Where am I going to be tomorrow? And
the day after tomorrow? In this place? I hope not!

3

Janet doesn't know where she is now. And she doesn't really
know where she is going to be tomorrow.

What about you?

Tomorrow I'm going to be in ___

The day after tomorrow I think I'm going to be in ___

Next month I'm probably going to be in ___

I hope I'm going to be in ___ next year/the year after that/in 19___

e

1

It is nine o'clock in the evening now. George is phoning Mr Snow at "The Park Hotel".

MR SNOW: Who are you? What's your name?

GEORGE: You don't think I'm going to tell you that, do you?

MR SNOW: Where's my daughter? When am I going to see her again?

GEORGE: Are you going to listen to me? Because if you aren't, I'm going to hang up.

MR SNOW: No. Don't hang up. I'm listening.

GEORGE: We want a million dollars from you. Tomorrow. And . . .

MR SNOW: I know that. But I haven't got a million dollars. Where am I going to find it?

GEORGE: That's your problem. But if you want your daughter, find it.

MR SNOW: But I can't give you the money tomorrow. Give me more time.

GEORGE: More time? How much more time? When can you give us the money?

MR SNOW: Probably the day after tomorrow.

GEORGE: Probably? No! Not probably! We want the money the day after tomorrow. And you are going to give us the money the day after tomorrow. Do you understand?

MR SNOW: All right, all right! I'm definitely going to give you the money the day after tomorrow.

GEORGE: Definitely?

MR SNOW: Yes! Definitely!

GEORGE: All right. The day after tomorrow. I'm going to hang up now.

MR SNOW: Wait! When are you going to phone again?

GEORGE: Tomorrow. At three in the afternoon. Goodbye. That's all now.

MR SNOW: But . . . but . . . *(George hangs up)*.

2

1. What does George want?
2. Why can't Mr Snow give George the money tomorrow?
3. When can he give him the money?
4. Is he definitely going to do this or is he probably going to do this?
5. What is George going to do tomorrow?

3

1. George wants __ __ __
2. But Mr Snow can't __ __ __ __ because __ __ __ __
3. George __ __ __ give him more __
4. Mr Snow is definitely __ __ __ __ __ __ the day after tomorrow.
5. George __ __ __ __ __ __ tomorrow __ three o'clock in the __

4

Lucky is asking George some questions. It is 10 pm, Sunday evening.

LUCKY: . . . ?

GEORGE: Yes, I did. I phoned him at nine o'clock.

LUCKY: . . . ?

GEORGE: No, he can't give us the money tomorrow.

LUCKY: . . . ?

GEORGE: Because he hasn't got it.

LUCKY: . . . ?

GEORGE: The day after tomorrow.

LUCKY: . . . ?

GEORGE: Yes, I am. Tomorrow. At 3 pm.

f

1

He She	**is**		**be** in America	
I	**am**	**going to**	**arrive** in London	on Friday.
You They We	**are**		**fly** to Dallas **meet** some friends **play** golf/tennis	next week. at ___ o'clock.

Is	he she		**be** in ___	
Am	I	**going to**	**arrive** in ___ **fly** to ___	on ___? next ___?
Are	you they we		**meet** some ___ **play** ___	at ___ o'clock?

→

Yes,	he she	**is.**
	I	**am.**
	you they we	**are.**

No,	he she	**isn't**.
	I	**'m not**.
	you they we	**aren't**.

2

Read this about Laura Francis

Laura got up at seven o'clock, as usual last Monday. First she had a shower. Then she had breakfast. After that she walked to the station. Her train came at eight fifteen.
She started work at nine and finished at half past five, as she always does.
On Monday and Wednesday Laura often meets some friends near Oxford Circus. They always meet at six and usually have dinner in an Indian or Italian restaurant. After that they usually go to a film or a concert.
It is Sunday evening now and Laura is thinking about what she is going to do tomorrow.

3

Speak and **Write**

(a) Laura is telling you what she is going to do tomorrow.
What is she saying?
1. Tomorrow/up/seven 2. Then/a shower
3. After that/breakfast 4. Then/the station
5. work/nine 6. five thirty 7. After work/some friends 8. We/a restaurant 9. After dinner/a film

(b) You don't know what Laura is going to do on Wednesday.
Ask her questions.

Are you going to . . . ?
Where/When are you going to . . . ?

1. your friends on Wednesday? 2. Where/dinner? 3. When/dinner? 4. a film on Wednesday, too? 5. Which film? 6. When/film start? 7. When/film finish?

What about you?

(c) What are you **probably** going to do tomorrow? What are you **definitely** going to do?

Can you write 6 sentences?

Tomorrow I am { **probably** / **definitely** } going to . . .

It is Monday morning, May 23rd. Janet is still in a small room in a factory in Camden Town. Of course, she doesn't want to stay there. But she can't leave. She has to stay there. She has to sit in that chair, too. She can't get up. Frank has to stay in the room, too. He has to watch her all the time.

Terry Carter has to get up early this morning. He has to take an examination today. He has to go to the University. But he is thinking about Janet.

TERRY: My God! I have to take an examination today. I have to answer a lot of questions. But how can I? Where's Janet? Is she all right?

Mr Snow is thinking about Janet, too. And he is thinking about money.

MR SNOW: A million dollars! I have to find a million dollars! The kidnappers want it tomorrow. I have to find it before tomorrow. But how am I going to do that?

In another part of London, a man is having breakfast. He has to go to work soon. And he has got a strange job. He has to wear those old clothes. Can you see them? People think he is a tramp. But he isn't really a tramp. He lives in a nice flat. His name is Tracey. Do you remember him? He is a detective.

a

PICTURE ONE

1. What do you think Janet wants to do?
2. Can she do it?
3. Why not?
4. *Talk about her and Frank*
   She has to . . .
   He has to . . .

PICTURE TWO

1. What is Terry going to do today?
2. Do you think he wants to take the exam today?
3. Why is he going to do it, then?
4. What is he thinking?

PICTURE THREE

Can you talk about Mr Snow, too?
   He has to . . .

PICTURE FOUR

1. Who is this man?
2. What kind of job has he got?
3. What is his name?
4. He has to do strange things in his job.
   What are they?

b

1

(*Stop and Look*)

She He	**has to**	**get up** soon.
		go to work/school/university.
		take an exam.
I We You They	**have to**	**answer** a lot of questions.
		find a million dollars.

2

Laura does these things every day. And she has to do them tomorrow.

   She gets up early = **She has to get up early tomorrow**.

1. She walks to the station.
2. She takes a train to work.
3. She starts at nine.
4. She works eight hours.
5. She does a lot of things.
6. She makes a lot of phone calls.
7. She types a lot of letters, too.

3   *Laura is talking to you.*
   What is she saying?

   I have to . . . tomorrow.

4

What about you?

What do you have to do every day?
What do you have to do tomorrow?
When do you have to . . . tomorrow?

   I have to . . . every day.
   I have to . . . tomorrow.
   Tomorrow I have to . . . at __ o'clock.

1

It is almost three o'clock in the afternoon.
George is going into a phone box.
What do you think he is going to do?
Who do you think he is going to phone?

What do you have to do when you make a phone call?
Do you know?

First, you lift the receiver, of course.

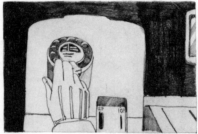

Then you put some money in the slot and then you dial the number.

When the person answers, you press the money in.

Do you understand all that? It's easy, isn't it?

George has got a cassette recorder with him.
He is going to play a cassette in a minute.
What do you have to do when you play a cassette?
Do you know?

First, of course, he is going to put the cassette in the recorder.

Then he is going to turn the recorder on. Can you see that switch? Is it on or off?

Then he is going to press the "play" button. That's easy, isn't it?

c

2

(a) *What is George going to do in the phone box?*

First he is going to . . .
Then . . .
After that . . .

(b) A friend from another country wants to use a telephone in England.
Tell your friend what he or she has to do

First you **have to** . . .
Then you **have to** . . .
After that . . .

(c) Now tell a friend about the cassette recorder.
What does he or she have to do first? And after that?

First you ___ to ___ a cassette in the ___
Then you ___ to ___ the recorder on.
After that . . .

(d) *What do you have to do when you record? Do you know?*

d

1

George is phoning Mr Snow again. *Listen*

GEORGE :   Have you got the money?

MR SNOW : Yes. What do I have to do now?

GEORGE :   Leave your hotel at seven o'clock this evening. Walk to Victoria Station.

MR SNOW : Walk? Why do I have to walk?

GEORGE :   Shut up and listen! No questions. Put the money in a black briefcase. Do you understand? Then go to the waiting room at Victoria. It's next to platform one. Be there at exactly seven twenty-five.

MR SNOW : And what do I have to do then?

GEORGE :   Go to the first telephone box next to the door and wait. Stand in the box.

MR SNOW : Wait a moment! How do I know my daughter is . . . I mean . . . perhaps she's dead.

GEORGE :   Shut up and listen! I've got a recording of her. Listen!

JANET :   Hello, dad. I don't know where I am. But I'm OK . . .

MR SNOW : Janet? Janet . . . . . . !

2

    He has to . . .

1. Mr Snow has to do something at seven o'clock. What?
2. He has to go somewhere. Where?
3. What about the money? What does he have to do with it?
4. Where does he have to be at seven twenty-five?
5. What does he have to do there?

3

1. At seven o'clock Mr Snow ___ to ___ the hotel.
2. He ___ ___ put the money in a ___ ___
3. At seven twenty-five he ___ ___ ___ to the waiting room at Victoria Station.
4. He ___ ___ ___ in the first telephone box next to the door.

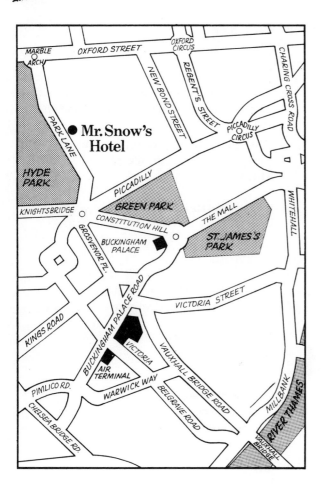

1 ⊙

Mr Snow wants to know how to get to Victoria Station. He is asking a clerk in the hotel. *Listen*

MR SNOW: Can you tell me how to get to Victoria Station?

CLERK: Well, you can take a taxi, sir. Or a bus.

MR SNOW: No, no! I'm walking there.

CLERK: Oh. Well . . . go out of the hotel and turn left. Walk down Park Lane to Hyde Park Corner. Turn left into Piccadilly. Walk up Piccadilly to Green Park. Then walk through Green Park . . . it's on your right. Buckingham Palace is straight ahead. Walk past Buckingham Palace to Buckingham Palace Road. Turn right and walk straight ahead to Victoria. You can't miss it.

MR SNOW: Uh . . . thanks.

CLERK: Can you remember all that?

MR SNOW: Uh . . . I . . . I think so. Yes.

2

But can Mr Snow really remember all that? He is talking to himself.
What is he saying?

MR SNOW: Now, let's see. When I *(1)* the hotel, I *(2)* to *(3)* left. Then I *(4)* to *(5)* down Park Lane. *(6)* I get to Hyde Park Corner I have to *(7)* *(8)* again. Then I *(9)* *(10)* *(11)* through Green Park. And then what? Oh! I can't remember!

Can you tell him?

Then you have to . . .

3

You are at Victoria Station.
Someone is asking you how to get to

a) the air terminal
b) Piccadilly Circus
c) Oxford Circus
d) Marble Arch
e) Vauxhall Bridge

Can you tell him or her how to get to these places?

> **Turn right/left . . .**
> **Go down/up . . .**
> etc.

or

> **You have to . . .**

f

Mr Snow **has to leave** at seven.
When **does** he **have to leave**? – At seven.

I **have to leave** at seven.
When **do** you **have to leave**? – At seven.

He **has to go** to Victoria Station.
Where **does** he **have to go**? – To Victoria Station.

I **have to go** to Victoria Station.
Where **do** you **have to go**? – To Victoria Station.

He **has to walk** there.
Does he **have to walk** there? – Yes, he **does**.

I **have to walk** there.
Do you **have to walk** there? – Yes, I **do**.

2

Let's talk about Laura again. She has to do these things every day. Do you remember?

1. She has to get up at seven.
2. She has to leave the house at eight.
3. She has to walk to the station.
4. She has to be there at eight fifteen.
5. She has to be at the travel agency at nine.

4

Now ask questions about her. What are the answers?

1. ___ does ___ have to ___ ___? – ___ seven.
2. ___ ___ she ___ ___ leave the ___? – ___ eight.
3. ___ she ___ ___ walk to the ___? – Yes, she ___
4. When ___ ___ ___ ___ ___ at the station? – ___ eight fifteen.
5. Where ___ ___ ___ ___ ___ at nine? – ___ ___ travel agency.

3

You are asking Laura questions

YOU: ___ do you ___ to get ___?
LAURA: At seven.
YOU: And ___ ___ ___ ___ ___ ___?
LAURA: Oh, about eight o'clock.
YOU: ___ ___ ___ ___ ___ to the station?
LAURA: Yes, I do. There isn't a bus, and I haven't got a car.
YOU: ___ ___ ___ ___ ___ ___ there?
LAURA: At eight fifteen. My train always comes then.
YOU: When ___ ___ have ___ be ___ ___ ___?
LAURA: At the agency? At nine.

5

What about you?

What do you have to do every day? When do you have to do it? Write

1. I usually ___ ___ ___ up at ___
2. On Monday I ___ ___ ___ to work/school at ___ o'clock.
3. So I ___ ___ ___ the house at ___

What are some other things you have to do on Tuesday, Wednesday, Thursday or Friday? Can you write about them?

On ___ I usually have to . . .

FOR EXTRA PRACTICE, SEE READ AND WRITE 5, PAGE 115

Goodbye

It is June now.
Flight 705 to New York is going to leave soon.

LOUDSPEAKER: Pan Am Airlines announces the departure of Flight seven oh five to New York. Passengers are requested to go to Gate Eleven immediately, where this flight is now boarding.

Janet is one of the passengers. She is saying goodbye to Terry.

JANET: Well, they're calling my flight now. I have to go.
TERRY: Goodbye, Janet. See you soon.
JANET: Yes, Terry. Soon. Very soon.

Frank Mitchum is back in prison. He is sitting in a cell. And he is thinking.

FRANK: Here I am, back in prison again. Why? Why did I listen to Lucky and George? Why didn't I find a job? My God! When am I going to get out of prison again? Perhaps never! Am I going to die in this place?

And George? What about George? He is in prison, too. He can't believe it.

GEORGE: I can't believe it. I have to get up at six every morning. I can't smoke cigars. I have to wear this terrible uniform. What happened? How did the police know?

a

PICTURE ONE

1. Which month is it now?
2. What can you see in the picture?
3. What are those people doing?
4. Where are they going?
5. What is the plane going to do?

PICTURE TWO

Ask and answer

1. Where . . . ?
2. Is Terry going to . . . ?
3. Is Janet going to . . . ?
4. Does she have to . . . ?
5. Does he have to . . . ?

PICTURE THREE

1. Is Frank going to America, too?
2. Where is he?
3. Do you think he is happy?
4. What are some of the things he is thinking?

PICTURE FOUR

You are speaking to George.
Ask him questions

1. ___ ___ happy?
2. Do you have to . . . ?
3. Can you . . . ?
4. Why do you have to . . . ?
5. Why can't you . . . ?

b

But what happened last month, on Monday, May 23rd?
Why are George and Frank in prison now?
Why isn't Lucky in prison, too?

1

Read this and find out

> Mr Snow left his hotel at exactly seven o'clock. Tracey was behind him. He followed Mr Snow to Victoria Station. It was seven twenty when Mr Snow got to the station. He went to the waiting room next to platform one. Then he went into the first telephone box next to the door. George phoned him at exactly seven twenty-five. Mr Snow lifted the receiver and listened. George told him exactly what to do.

2

EXAMPLE: When ___ Mr Snow ___ his hotel?
= **When did Mr Snow leave his hotel?**
At exactly seven o'clock.

1. ___ Tracey behind him?
2. ___ he ___ him to Victoria Station?
3. When ___ they ___ to the station?
4. Where ___ Mr Snow ___ then?
5. When ___ George ___ him?
6. What ___ Mr Snow ___ then?

3

You are Mr Snow. What did you do that evening last month?

1

But what did George tell Mr Snow to do? *Listen*

MR SNOW: What do I have to do now?

GEORGE: Walk to Vauxhall Bridge.

MR SNOW: Vauxhall Bridge? Where's that?

GEORGE: It's at the end of Vauxhall Bridge Road.

MR SNOW: But where's Vauxhall Bridge Road?

GEORGE: It's very near the station. Ask a policeman! Now listen! When you get to Vauxhall Bridge Road, turn right. Walk down the road. Stay on the right and stay near the kerb! Very near the kerb. Don't cross the road. Have you got that?

MR SNOW: Go to Vauxhall Bridge Road. Turn right. Don't cross the road. Walk down the road to the bridge. Yes. I understand. What do I have to do when I get to the bridge?

GEORGE: Wait there! One more thing. Do the police know about this?

MR SNOW: Of course they don't.

GEORGE: Good. Because if they *do*, you're never going to see your daughter again!

MR SNOW: Is she all right? When *am* I going to see her again?

GEORGE: No more questions now. We want the money first! Have you got it?

MR SNOW: Of course I have.

GEORGE: And is it in a black briefcase?

MR SNOW: Yes, it is. But . . .

GEORGE: That's all now. Goodbye.

2

It is Monday evening, May 23rd.
It is seven twenty-five.
What does Mr Snow have to do now?

Where does Mr Snow have to . . .
Does he have to . . .
What does he have to do when he . . .

3

What do these words and phrases in the dialogue mean?

EXAMPLE: Vauxhall Bridge? Where's *that*?
   "that" = Vauxhall Bridge.

1. "Wait *there*."
2. "Do the police know about *this*?"
3. "Of course they *don't*."
4. "Good, because if they *do*, you're never going to see your daughter again."

4

It is June now.
What did Mr Snow do that evening last month?

First he left the hotel. Then he ___ to Victoria Station. After that he . . .
etc.

Mr Snow is telling you about that evening last month.
What is he saying?

MR SNOW: First I ___ my hotel. Then I . . .
   etc.

d

1 🎧 *And what happened then? Look at the pictures. Can you tell the story?*

After Mr Snow left the station, he walked to Vauxhall Bridge Road. He turned right and walked down the road. There was a lot of traffic. He stayed very near the kerb.

But Mr Snow didn't walk to the bridge. Before he got there, a man came up the road on a motorbike. It was Lucky. He grabbed the briefcase from Mr Snow. And of course all the money was in the briefcase. Mr Snow didn't see Lucky's face. Lucky had a helmet on.

Tracey was behind Mr Snow. Lucky didn't see him. But Tracey saw Lucky. He didn't see his face, either. But he saw the licence number of the motorbike. And he remembered it. Tracey had a small radio in his pocket.

2

Did . . . ?
Where was . . . ?
Why didn't . . . ?
What did ___ do?
Did ___ have a ___?

3

What do you think?

What did Tracey do with the radio?

Did he ⎰ listen to Marty Davis?
speak to the police?
speak to Mr Snow?
speak to Frank Mitchum at the old factory?
give the police the licence number?

I'm sure he didn't . . .
I think he probably . . .
Perhaps he . . .

▌ ☺ *And what happened then?*

After Lucky grabbed the money, he drove to the old factory near the canal in Camden Town. But he didn't know that the police had his licence number. You see, Tracey gave them the number. He spoke to them on his small pocket radio.

Three police cars followed Lucky. Of course, it was never the same police car. But one car was always in radio contact with the other two.

When Lucky got to the old factory, a policewoman saw him. She was on a bridge near the canal. She had a small pocket radio, too. Now the police knew exactly where Janet was.

Twenty minutes later the police broke into the old factory. Frank was there. George and Lucky were there, too. And of course Janet was there. The police freed her and arrested George and Frank. But they didn't arrest Lucky. Why not?

A minute before the police came, Lucky went to the toilet. He was there when the police came. He heard them, of course. The toilet was on the side of the factory near the canal. He climbed out of a small window, jumped into the canal and swam to the other side. And then he ran away.

f

1

You are a) Lucky Jones
b) a policeman
c) Mr Snow

Tell your side of the story

LUCKY: After I . . . , I . . . Then I
. . . I . . . When I was . . .
the police . . . They
didn't . . . because I . . . .

POLICEMAN: Three of our cars . . .
all the time. One of
our policewomen . . .
Twenty minutes later
we . . . We arrested
. . . but we didn't . . .
because . . .

MR SNOW: After Lucky . . . , they
. . . Of course I never
knew that . . . Lucky
and George took me
to . . . Twenty minutes
later . . . The police
. . . us and . . . George
and Frank. But . . .

2 ⊚ *What is going to happen to these people now?*
Listen and find out!

Janet is going to come back to England next September. She is
going to live in Camden Town again.
Terry isn't sure what he is going to do. Perhaps he is going to
find a job in Manchester. Or perhaps he is going to work in
London. He doesn't know.
And Frank and George? They're going to be in prison for a
long time!

3 But what about you? What are you going to do? Where are
you going to be next year? Do you know?

Speak and write about yourself

Next month I'm going to . . .
I'm going to . . . next year.

I'm not sure/I don't know {**what** / **where**} **I'm going to . . .**

I'm probably going to . . .

a
At the airport

Here is an announcement

Flight	Time of departure	Destination	Gate
L H 121	0930	FRANKFURT	12
SR 343	1015	ZURICH	9
AF 729	1045	PARIS	11
SA 309	1000	STOCKHOLM	3
OA 662	1030	ATHENS	19

Lufthansa announce the departure of Flight LH121 to Frankfurt. This flight is leaving from Gate twelve. This is the Lufthansa nine thirty flight to Frankfurt.

Write an announcement for the second flight. (This is a Swissair flight.)

Now answer these questions about the third flight

1. What time is Flight AF729?
2. Where is Flight AF729 going to?
3. Which gate is it leaving from?

You can see two other flights. Ask and answer questions about them

b This is Janet's family

New York — Howard Snow

Nancy Snow — Boston

London

Janet Snow

Larry Snow — San Francisc[o]

Howard Snow is Janet's father. He lives in New York. Nancy Snow is Janet's mother. She lives in Boston. They have two children, Janet and Larry.

Larry is Janet's brother. She hasn't got a sister. Janet lives in London. She's single. She's not married.

Write about Larry

Janet __ Larry's __.
He hasn't got __ __.
Larry __ __ San Francisc[o]
He's not married. He's __

c Janet Snow is talking about herself:

I was born in New York on the 26th of October, 1958. This is my second visit to London. I'm staying at the Park Hotel in Park Lane. My passport number is Z930657

Fill in Janet's embarkation card

SURNAME (1)	FIRST NAME (2)
PASSPORT NO (3)	
PLACE AND DATE OF BIRTH (4)	
ADDRESS IN UK (5)	

What about you ?

d

**Janet is staying
at the Park Hotel**

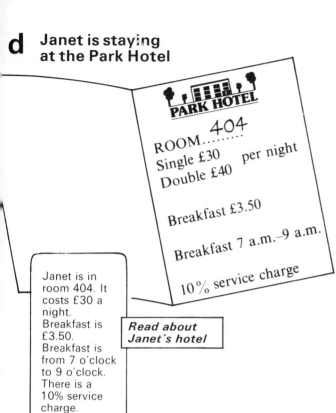

PARK HOTEL

ROOM 404
Single £30
Double £40 per night

Breakfast £3.50

Breakfast 7 a.m.–9 a.m.

10% service charge

Janet is in room 404. It costs £30 a night. Breakfast is £3.50. Breakfast is from 7 o'clock to 9 o'clock. There is a 10% service charge.

Read about Janet's hotel

**Terry is staying
at York House**

York House

ROOM. 16.

Single £5.00
Double £7.50
(including breakfast)

Breakfast 7.30 – 9 o'clock

Terry — —
Room —. It costs —. Breakfast — included. Breakfast is from — to —. There is — service charge.

Write about Terry's hotel

This is Janet's bill

PARK HOTEL

Park Lane, London W.1.

Room No 404

Name Miss Janet Snow

Room	£90.00
Meals	£10.50
Drinks	£ 7.50
Newspapers	50
Extras	
+ 10% service	£10.85
TOTAL	£119.35

Look at this cheque

Centre Bank ✳ 3 October   19

Pay Franco's Restaurant

the sum of Five pounds 60p   £5—60
       only

JANET SNOW   J. Snow

You are Janet.
Write the cheque and pay the hotel bill

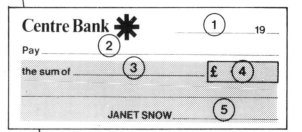

Centre Bank ✳   ①   19

Pay   ②

the sum of   ③   £ ④

JANET SNOW   ⑤

READ AND WRITE 2

a
Look at the morning programme for Radio Thames

Ask and answer

1. What's on at seven o'clock?
2. When does the first programme finish?
3. What can you hear on this programme?

Now ask and answer questions about the third and fifth programmes

Radio THAMES medium 1457 kHz/206m VHF 94.9 MHz **MONDAY October 3**

Marty Davis

Kevin Mason

Linda Gage

7.0 Good morning! It's Marty Davis! Music from Thames's top DJ

9.0 Thames News and Weather

9.15 London Today Linda Gage goes out and about to meet interesting people

10.00 Now Hear This! Tony Jordan with the best of the new records

12.00 London Folk News and music from the capital's folk scene Introduced by Kevin Mason

b
Accommodation to let

Foreign students in London usually live in flats or bedsitters. Sometimes they share them. In other words, they live in them with other people. And sometimes they live in "student hostels" (a kind of hotel for students) or in boarding houses. In a boarding house you get meals, too. You can see advertisements for flats, rooms and other places to live in the evening newspapers.

Can you understand the advertisements here?

ACCOMMODATION TO LET

B & B in boarding house from £12. Evening meals. Tel 774 5586

B/B £3 NIGHTLY, £14 p.w. Mermaid Hotel, 124 King's Road, S.W.3 234 8565

COMFORTABLE ROOM, c.h., breakfast. Central. £11.50 p.w. 504 6650 after 6.30.

STUDENT holiday accommodation special winter terms with or without breakfast. Phone Nash's Hotel 656 5892

WELL FURN. double room. Refs. 26 Lansdowne Place, W.1. 451 6512

SHARE BEAUTIFUL FLAT, own room, £55 p.m. Suit single guy. 723 3476

LARGE DOUBLE FLATLET, sep. kit., w.c., bath., £19 wk. Phone 776 7389 after 7.30 p.m.

FURN. S/C gr.f. flat. £40 p.c.m. Phone after 6 p.m. 722 8591

STUDENT BEDSITS from £10 p.w. H.C. Tel 242 6152

TWO double flatlets, one with separate kitchen, cooking facilities, £12 685 7673

Accommodation to let: flats, houses, etc. You pay rent for them.

B and B:	Bed and breakfast	**w.c.:**	water closet or toilet
p.w.:	per week		
p.m.:	per month	**s.c.:**	self contained. In other words the flat has got kitchen, bathroom and toilet in it.
p.c.m.:	per calendar month (not only four weeks)		
c.h.:	central heating (radiators)	**suit:**	is right for
		gr.f.:	ground floor

A student called Françoise lives in the room in the third advertisement.

Write about her

Françoise __ in a __ room.
The room __ __ central heating.
She __ £11.50 a __ for this __.

Look at the advertisement for the furnished self-contained flat. A student named Rolf lives in this flat. *What can you write about him?*

109

c

Here is an enrolment form for the Camden English Centre

Fill it in for Maria and Nobuo

1
Maria Risi is Italian. She's twenty-two. She lives at 48 Highbury Grove. She wants to stay at the Centre for four weeks. She doesn't want to learn English all the time. She wants time to do other things too.

2
Nobuo Sato is Japanese. He's thirty-five. He lives at 17 Randolph Street. His telephone number is 485 2132. He can only stay at the Centre for two weeks. He wants to learn a lot of English in two weeks.

3
What about you?

I am __ (nationality). I am __ (age).

I want to $\begin{Bmatrix} \text{— in England} \\ \text{— to England} \end{Bmatrix}$ for __ __.

d

Mike Sutton teaches at the Camden English Centre. This is a letter from one of his students to a new pen friend

You are Carlos' penfriend.
Write a letter to Carlos about yourself.

Tell him about

1. your school and/or job
2. where you come from
3. where you live
4. your family (how many brothers and sisters)

CAMDEN ENGLISH CENTRE

Fill in and send to:

Secretary, Camden English Centre, 158 Camden High St, London NW1.

Family name.................. First name(s)...............

Nationality..............Age........ Male/Female

London address..

Telephone number..............

How many hours of English do you want? ☐6☐ ☐15☐ ☐30☐
(please tick ✓)   hours a week

How many weeks of English do you want? ☐2☐ ☐4☐ ☐8☐ ☐12☐
(please tick ✓)

I wish to reserve a place at the Camden English Centre.
I enclose a deposit of £20

Signature........................ Date..................

14 Pratt St,
London NW 1.

14th November.

Dear Penfriend,

My name is Carlos Gomez. I come from Caracas in Venezuela and I am a student at the Camden English Centre. It is a language school in Camden Town, in London. I like it here. The classes are small. There are four other students in my class. They are friendly and they come from different countries. One comes from Paris in France. There are two women from Germany. And there is a man from Saudi Arabia. I am the fifth student.

My teacher's name is Mike Sutton. I like him, too. He is a good teacher. We have three classes in the morning with him. We have two classes in the afternoon, too. We have a different teacher then.

In Venezuela I work in a travel agency. American tourists often come to the agency. Usually they don't speak Spanish. And that is why I am learning English now.

I live with my family in Caracas in a flat. My mother works in a bank and my father works in a factory. I have got a brother and a sister, too. He is sixteen and she is twenty-one. My sister goes to university. She is very intelligent. She is studying medicine. My brother is not very intelligent and he was very bad at school. But he has got a job now in a garage. He is a mechanic there. He loves cars.

Well all this is about me. But what about you? Please write. Tell me about yourself.

Yours sincerely
Carlos.

a

This is from a brochure at Laura's travel agency in Camden Town. It is easy to get to Paris from London and people often go there for "a short break".

Peter Norris is going to Paris with his son, Simon. Simon is under 12. They want to stay in a good hotel for two nights (from Saturday to Monday). Peter wants a private bathroom.
How much does he pay?

Janet wants to go to Paris for four nights. She wants a very good hotel. She wants a single room with a private bathroom.
How much does she pay?

What about you?

You want "a short break" in Paris, too.
How long do you want to stay?
What kind of hotel do you want?
Do you want a private bathroom, too?
How much does all this cost?

Book now. Write a short letter to Travel Centre, Camden High Street, London NW1.

Start: *Dear Sir,*
Finish: *Yours faithfully*

Say what you want, how long you want to stay, etc.

TAKE A SHORT BREAK IN PARIS

PRICE CHART

| | Bed and Breakfast | | |
| | * | ** | *** |
	£ p	£ p	£ p
2 nights in Paris	53.10	58.10	67.90
3 nights in Paris	57.50	65.00	79.70
4 nights in Paris	61.90	71.90	91.50
5 nights in Paris	66.30	78.80	103.30

	*	**	***
Extra for private bathroom per person a night	2.70	3.50	—
Extra for single room per night	2.20	4.00	5.20
Extra for single room & private bathroom per night	6.50	9.00	5.20

Note

Prices include travel by Air France or British Airways from London to Paris. You can leave any day of the week *if you spend Saturday night in Paris.*

Reduction of £20.00 for children under 12.

Accommodation is in one, two or three star hotels with breakfast. All hotels are clean and in or near the centre of Paris. Service charges and taxes are included in the prices.

*   Good. Hot and cold water in every room. No lift.

**   Very good. Lift. Telephone in all rooms.

*** First class. Very comfortable. Colour TV in all rooms. Telephone, lift, etc.

b

Look at this.
It is from the
Camden Times

Now answer the questions

1. The Camden Times thinks two films are very good. Which two films?
2. You want to go and see a film. You only have £1.20. Which cinemas can you go to?
3. It is one o'clock. You want to see a film now. Which film are you going to?
4. You're taking your brother to the cinema. He wants to see a war film. Which cinema can you go to?

```
  *   = Bad
 **   = Fair
 ***  = Good
 **** = Very good
```

CLASSIC
The Sheriff****
3.40, 6.00, 8.20
Late show Fri and Sat 11.00
Seats £1.20, £1.80

ABC
Star in the Night***
3.25, 5.55, 8.30
Late show Sat 11.30
Seats £1.20

GRANADA
The City is Burning**
1.15, 4.30, 7.45
Late show Sat 11.15
Seats £1

C

This is a letter from Janet's father to Janet

10 Waterside Plaza,
New York
N.Y 10610.
January 25

Dear Janet,

I am in my new apartment now. It is very nice. I have got a beautiful view of the river. I hope you can come and stay here next year.

It is very cold here. In fact, it is snowing. I can't stand snow, either.

In a few weeks I am going to Saudi Arabia. I am going on business. It is hot there now. No snow! Perhaps I can stop and see you in London on the way.

I see your mother sometimes, but not very often. Do you write to her? I hope so. She is happy now, I think. I am happy now, too. This is the best thing for her and for me. I hope you understand.

Love,
Dad

Look at the envelope, too!

By air mail
Par avion

USA 21c
UNITED STATES AIR MAIL

Miss Janet Snow,
58 Albert Gardens,
London N.W.3,
England.

Ask and answer

1. Where ___?
2. Has he got _____?
3. Is it __ in New York now?
4. Does he like __?
5. Is he going to __ __ in a few weeks?
6. ___ there on business?
7. __ hot there?
8. __ stop in __ on the __?
9. __ Mr Snow live __ Mrs Snow?
10. __ happy now?

Write out envelopes for these three people. Use:

Mr   Mrs or **Miss**

1. Janet's father. His full name is Howard Snow and his address is in his letter.
2. Janet's mother, Nancy Snow. She lives at 3445 Rowley Avenue, Boston, Mass., U.S.A.
3. Laura Francis. Her address is 69 Woodland Road, Watford, Herts, England.

EON
Last Bridge**
), 5.20, 8.20
ts £1.50, £2

RLTON
od and the Vampire****
), 6.15, 8.40
ts £1.50, £1.85, £2.20

AZA
gh Now, Pay Later*
), 4.15, 6.00, 8.15
ts £1.20, £1.50

a

THE BELL

The Bell is the pub near the Camden English Centre. Mike Sutton goes to it. So do many other teachers and students from the Centre. It's their "local". It's a friendly place and it's always busy.

Len Franklin is the landlord of The Bell. He likes his job but he works very hard. Pubs in Britain are not open all day. From Monday to Saturday they are open for eight or nine hours every day. The Bell opens at eleven in the morning and stays open until three o'clock in the afternoon. Then it opens again from six o'clock until eleven o'clock. On Sundays it closes at half past ten.

In Britain, children cannot go into pubs. After the age of 14 they can go in with an adult, but they cannot drink alcohol. In The Bell, there is a sign in the bar. It says:

Sorry!
We don't serve anyone under 18

Len Franklin likes children. He has got two children himself. But he doesn't like children in his pub. "People come here to talk and have a quiet drink," he says. "They don't want children in here. They make too much noise."

Ask and answer:

Where _ _ _? = Where is The Bell? – It is near the Camden English Centre.
1. Do students _ _?
2. Do teachers _ _, too?
3. Who is the landlord _ _?
4. Does he _ _?
5. Are pubs _ all day?
6. When do they _?
7. _ _ close?
8. Can children under 14 _ _ _?
9. _ _ over 14 _ _?
10. _ children over 14 _ alcohol?

What about your country?

1. Have you got pubs or bars in your country?
2. If you haven't, where can you drink coffee or tea in the evening?
3. How long are these places open?
4. When do they open and close?
5. What can you drink in them?
6. Can children under 14 go into them? What do they drink?

Start In my country _

b

Frank Mitchum looked at these advertisements for jobs in the paper. Can you understand them?

£70 A WEEK Young and beauti staff for late night restaurant. Pho 936-7801

COOK Saudi Arabia, 170 m from Jeddah. Salary £450 pm, free. Free accommodation a food. Two trips home a year w return air fare paid. For more in mation phone Mr Cardin 507 10

CLERK IN TRAVEL AGEN Good chance for intelligent you man or woman 18–25. 485 5677

MENSWEAR SALESPERS 5-day week. 3 weeks hoilday. Go wages. Apply KENT'S MEN WEAR 16/18 CAMDEN HIG STREET or phone 387 4417

FULL TIME SALES ASSISTA for boutique. Experience necessa £50–£60 p.w. For interview ph SALLY SPENCE 581 8181

Are you a young man or wom between 18 and 40? Can you sp a foreign language? Do you w to travel? Can you work long ho for very good pay? Have you go driving licence? We are a big in national organisation and we looking for people like you. W to Box 790 for more informatio

Which jobs aren't right for Frank?

This job isn't right for him because

he $\begin{cases} \text{can't } \ldots \\ \text{isn't } \ldots \\ \text{hasn't got experience in this kind of job.} \end{cases}$

What about you?

Which jobs are right? Which jobs are wrong for you? Why?

You have to interview a person in your class for one of these jobs.

Ask questions like:

How old __ __? Can you __? Do you __?
Have you got __ __? Are you __?

Can you ask more questions?

THE CAMDEN TIMES

THURSDAY, APRIL 14, 19

SALES STAFF male or female. Large department store in Oxford Street. No experience necessary. Good wages. Please ring 836 6030

Secretary, part time or full time. Phone Mr Belsen 485 2734

BARPERSON wanted for famous Camden Town pub. Good wages. 5½ days a week. Apply in person to The Bell, Camden High Street.

Teacher of English as a Foreign Language. University degree or Diploma in EFL necessary. Salary to £5,500 a year. Apply Pamela Hilary, Camden English Centre, Camden High Street, LONDON NW1

Young person wanted for Camden Town supermarket. 18–21. No experience necessary. Ring Mr Petchey, 485 3271

Vocabulary

Salary: pay, usually every month

Wages: pay, usually by the hour

Experience: if you worked in this kind of job before, you have got experience

Necessary: if you haven't got this, you cannot get the job. It is necessary

Staff: the people working in a shop, office, school or factory are the staff

What are the other words you can't understand?

Ask your teacher

What does __ mean?

---

14 Burbage Street,

LONDON SW3.

15th April, 19..

Box 790,
The Camden Times,
LONDON NW1.

Dear Sir,

I saw your advertisement yesterday and I would like some more information.

What kind of work is it and where is your office? What are the hours and how much is the salary?

I am 26 years old and I work in an international bank. I can speak French and German. I have also got a driving licence. I want to travel and use my foreign languages. I can come to an interview next week.

Yours faithfully,

Susan Blake

Susan Blake

C

This is an answer to one of these advertisements. *Which advertisement?*

What about you?

Can you write a letter for this job, too? Give your name and other information. What questions do you ask about the job?

a

Transport in London

If you want to travel by public transport in London, you can go by "tube" (the Underground) or you can go by bus. There are two kinds of bus. Double-deckers and single-deckers. The double-deckers usually have got a driver and a conductor. You get on, and then you sit down. After that the conductor takes your fare. But on the single-deckers you pay when you get on. There are no conductors. You put your fare in a box behind the driver. The fare is always the same. But on the double-deckers, the fares are different.

On the double-deckers you can't stand on top. You can only sit. And on the bottom deck, only five people can stand when all the seats are full. In the rush hour the buses are often full. The conductor often says "Sorry, full up!" This means you can't get on. Or perhaps he says "Only two seats on top!"

In the rush hour the tube is very crowded, too. Perhaps you can get a seat. But you usually stand. When people get on, they push and shove. There are eight main lines – the Northern Line, the Central Line and so on. At some stations you can change from one line to another. And the fares are all different.

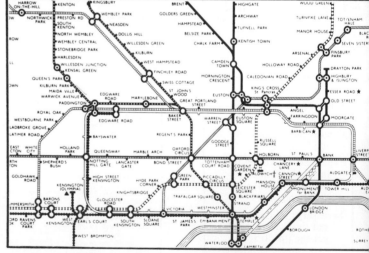

Write and speak

1. You live in London. Your friend doesn't. But he or she is coming to London. Tell your friend about
   a) the two kinds of buses
   b) the fares on these buses
   c) the rush hour and what the conductor says, etc.

2. You live in Camden Town. Your friend is arriving at Victoria Station. How can your friend get to Camden Town by tube? You are writing to him or her. What do you say? (Look at the Underground map!)

   Take the __ __ to __ __ Then change at __ __ Get off at __ __

3. Ali is a student in London. He lives near Queensway and he goes to the Camden English Centre in Camden Town. How does he travel by tube every day?

   He __ the Central Line to __ __ __ Then he __ at __ __ __ and __ __ __ __ __ to __ __

The London Transport Collection

Syon Park
Brentford
Middlesex

The London Transport Collection

of old buses, trams, trolley-buses, posters, signs, tickets and other exhibits — is open every day at Syon Park, Brentford.

Opening times:

10 00 – 18 00

Admission 40p (children 25p)

Underground to Hammersmith, then bus 267. Or to Gunnersbury, then buses 237 or 267. On Sundays buses E1 and E2 run beyond Brentford to Syon Park.
British Rail to Syon Lane, then walk.

b
This is an advertisement for one of the museums in London

Look at it. Then answer the questions

1. What kind of things can you see in this museum?
2. You want to go to this museum and you haven't got a car. You live in the centre of London. What do you have to do?
3. When can you see the collection (all the things there)?
4. Last Saturday you and a friend went to this museum. Write a postcard to another friend about it.

Post Card

Last Saturday ——— the London Transport Collection. We ——— a 267 bus ——— the museum. ——— buses, trams and trolley-buses there.
Goodbye for now,

c
Which signs go with which words?

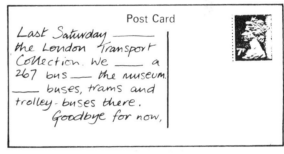

1 Airport	2 Gentlemen	3 No entry
4 No smoking	5 Food served here	6 Telephone

a · d · b · e · c · f

d
Which sentence goes with which picture?

a) You can't go out this way. Use the other door.
b) Excuse me, sir, but you can't stand here. There are some seats below.
c) Hey! Don't go in there!
d) Stop! You're going into a one way street.
e) Don't you know this is a non-smoker?

Review

Unit 1

1

What's (What is)	**the** time? **your** name?	**It** **My** name	's **is**	one o'clock. Anna Parker.

2

Where's (Where is)	Chicago? Leeds?	It's **in**	America. England.

3

Is	London New York Mike Anna	in **from**	America? England?	Yes, No,	**he** **she** it	**is**. **isn't**.

4

Where	**are you** **is he/she**	from?	**I'm (I am)** He's (He is) She's (She is)	from	Frankfurt. Rio. Madrid.

PLUS   **This** is London.
London is **a** city **too**.
Look! Look at Anna **and** Mike!
Pardon?
Thank you.
Numbers 1–6.

Unit 2

1

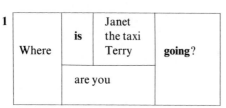

Where	**is** are you	Janet the taxi Terry	**going**?

2

Terry Janet The taxi It/He/She I'm	is	going **to**	London. the airport. New York.

3

Is	Janet the plane Terry	going to	New York?	Yes, No,	he she it	is. isn't.

4

I'm not (I am not) Anna isn't (is not)	**at** the airport. **on** the plane.

5

Is	this **that**	your	suitcase? bag?	No,	this that	is my	suitcase. bag.

PLUS   **Here** you are.
His name is George.
Call **me** a taxi, please.
Here's my ticket.
Put your suitcase on the scale, please.
Numbers 7–18

Unit 3

1

They're (They are)	near Watford. at the station. on the train.

2

His Her	train	is at platform 7.
The train to London		

3

What time Which platform	is	the train to London?	6.40. Platform 4.
How much		a single to London?	£12.

4

Look at	**this** **that**	woman.

PLUS Excuse me. He is buying a ticket. She is speaking to Terry.
     Numbers 19, 20, 30, 40, 50, 60

Unit 4

1

We're (We are) They're	**over**	London New York	now.

2

I You	**can** see	Big Ben. Janet.

3

Can you see	the plane? the train?

4

Who's (Who is) that? It's	George. the taxi-driver.

PLUS Here's Janet, but **what about** George?
     Can you see **him**?
     No smoking, please.
     One picture is on the right, **the other** picture is on the left.

Unit 5

1

I You We They	**have** **haven't**	**got**	my your his her **their**	cigars. suitcases. shirts. car. ticket.
He She	**has** **hasn't**		**an**	umbrella.

2

Have	I/you we/they	got	a skirt? a pair **of** jeans?	Yes, No,	I/you we/they	have. haven't.
Has	he/she		a camera? a newspaper?		he/she	has. hasn't.

3

He's She's	a	porter. policeman. clerk. policewoman.

4

The porter Anna Mike	is	listening to waiting **for** looking at	**them.** him. **her.**

5

What	are they is she	**doing?**	They're She's	waiting for	their her	tickets. friends.

6

How many	boxes of cigars bottles of whisky pairs of jeans	have you got?	I've got	2. 3. 20.

PLUS My hotel is **between** a pub and a garage.

It's a **small** hotel.

It's **cheap** too.

How many suitcases have you got? **Only one. This one.**

Have you got **these** things too?

Numbers 70–150

Unit 6

1

There	**isn't** **is**	a light a chair	near the door. in this room.
	are **aren't**	two beds 200 rooms	in this hotel. **next to** the window.

2

Is Are	there	a shower a washbasin	in her room? in the bathroom?	Yes, No,	there	is. isn't.
		three beds ten cigars	in this room? in that box?			are. aren't.

3

How many	tables windows doors	are there here?	There	is	one.
				are	four.

4

Can	he you Janet	see	them? the hotel? her?	Yes,	he I they we	**can.**
				No,		**can't.**

PLUS **How long** are you staying, sir?

Are **those** Miss Snow**'s** suitcases? No, they aren't – they're Terry's suitcases.

It's a **very** small hotel.

Have I got a room **with** a bathroom?

Unit 7

1

I He She You	can can't	drive. cook. dance. swim.

2			
Can you	play tennis? ski?	Yes, I can, but not very well.	

PLUS Can you speak **any** foreign languages?
Terry/Janet is looking for a room **like** this.
Where is it? What's the address, **I mean**?

Unit 8

1
He She	**lives** **works**	there. in a hotel.
They You I We	**live** **work**	in this block of flats. **under our** flat. in America. **behind** the school.

2
Do	they you	live near a park? work in an office?	Yes, No,	they I we	**do.** **don't.**
Does	he she			he she	**does.** **doesn't.**

PLUS They **are having** lunch.
How are you? How do you do?

Unit 9

1
He She	**often** **never** **usually** **always** **sometimes**	gets up at . . . has breakfast at . . . goes to work at . . .
I/You We/They		get up at . . . have breakfast at . . . go to work at . . .

2
When	do	you	get up? have breakfast? go to work/school?
	does	he she	have lunch/dinner? get home? go to bed?

PLUS **I think/I know** she leaves at nine.
I don't know. No, thanks, I don't smoke.
She . . . **in the morning/on Monday/at** . . . o'clock/**every day.**
Sometimes she doesn't have lunch at all.

Unit 10

1

Anna Terry	**doesn't**	live in . . . work in . . . go to . . .
I You We They	**don't**	know . . . own . . . smoke . . . play . . . have breakfast at . . .

PLUS **I'm sure** he's a burglar!
George earns **a lot of** money.
He earns £40,000 **a** year.
He wants **more**.
No more questions, please.

Unit 11

1

I **want**	**some** peas. a cup of coffee.
He **wants**	a glass of red wine. **some** tea.

2

She doesn't	**like**	prison food. pizza.
They don't		grapefruit. salami.

3

I don't want **any**	beer, potatoes, ice cream,	thank you.

4

Have you got any	fried rice? boiled potatoes? chips?

PLUS They**'re having** lunch now.
What kind of pizza do you want?
Do you want **anything** to drink?
I'd like some coffee, please.
Look at the time – **let's go**.
I **want to** pay for my pizza.

Unit 12

1

He She	**wants to**	go to the cinema. have a drink.
I/You We/They	**want to**	go to the zoo. watch television.

2

Yes, **let's**	go to the cinema. have a drink. go to the zoo. watch television.

3

The fare to America is	£220	**before** **after**	June 1st. September 30th.

PLUS **We'd like** some information, please.

The air fare is £220 – it's **more** in August, but it's **less** in March.

Where do they want to go? **When** do they want to go?

What else is on?

Unit 13

1

She He I	**was** **wasn't**	at home in prison in Manchester	yesterday. last month. last week. in 1965.
You They We	**were** **weren't**	in Kuwait at school	

2

Was	Anna Frank I	tired hungry free	this morning? last Thursday? at 10.00 yesterday? yesterday evening?	Yes, No,	she he I	was. wasn't.
Were	you we those men	in prison **outside** the school at the teacher's house			you we they	were. weren't.

3

Why do you want to	talk to see meet	me?	**Because** I've got	**something** a job some money	for you.

PLUS Past tense: work   follow   start   see   come   go   leave

worked   **followed**   **started**   **saw**   **came**   **went**   **left**

He started school **when** he was five.

He **was born** in . . .

Unit 14

1

I You We He She They	**had** lunch in Leeds **bought** that newspaper **got** a new job **worked** in Bristol **earned** £200 **typed** ten letters	yesterday. on Monday. yesterday evening. last December. last week. last year.

2

Did	they you he	live work	in	London Paris Berlin	last year? before 1978? after 1975?	Yes, No,	they I he	**did.** **didn't.**

PLUS Which subjects did you study/like?

Do you mind if I ask some questions?

That was **before** I got this job.

It wasn't very **interesting**.

Unit 15

1

When did you	get up have breakfast go to school	yesterday?

2				
What did	you Frank	eat do see	**before** **after**	breakfast? that? you went to work? he came home?

3			
Do you mind if I	smoke? sit down? open the window?		No, that's all right.

PLUS **Someone** wants to talk to you.
He left her **about** midnight.
Are you **interested**?

Unit 16

1			
He She I You We They	**didn't**	go to the cinema answer the phone see a film have breakfast run in Regent's Park	last week. yesterday. at 3.00 on Monday.

2			
Why didn't	you he	go home? see that film?	Because . . .

3								
He	usually	gets up at 7.30 has lunch at 12.30	but	I he	didn't	get up have lunch	at . . . this morning.
I		get up at 8.30 have lunch at 1.15					

PLUS **Don't** shout.
Get **into** the van.
I think he's **going to** stay in a hotel.
I don't think he's going to give me a million dollars.

Unit 17

1			
I'm You're We're It's They're He's	**going to**	arrive shave rain take off watch TV get home	tomorrow afternoon. at nine o'clock. this evening. in a minute. next week. the day after tomorrow.

PLUS Tomorrow I **think** I'm going to be in . . .
I **hope** I'm going to be in . . . next year.
Next month I'm **probably** going to . . .
He's **definitely** going to . . .

Unit 18

1

| I
You
We
The police | **have to** | get off here.
give George the money.
get up early today.
pay the bill. |
| Mr Snow
Laura | **has to** | find Janet.
get a million dollars. |

2

| **Do** | I
you
we
the police | **have to** | get off
give it to him
get up
pay it | now? | Yes,
No, | you
I
we
they | **do.**
don't. |
| **Does** | Mr Snow
Laura | | find her
get it | | | he
she | **does.**
doesn't. |

3

| Can you tell me **how to get to** . . .? | **First** . . . **Then** . . . **After that** . . . |

PLUS **Turn right/left. Walk down** Park Lane. **Go up** Piccadilly.
Walk **past** Buckingham Palace. **You can't miss it.**

Goodbye   Revision of **going to do** and PAST TENSE.

Days, months, numbers

Days of the week

Sunday, Monday, Tuesday, Wednesday, Thursday, Friday, Saturday

Months of the year

January, February, March, April, May, June, July, August, September, October, November, December

Numbers

1 one	11 eleven	21 twenty-one
2 two	12 twelve	22 twenty-two
3 three	13 thirteen	30 thirty
4 four	14 fourteen	40 forty
5 five	15 fifteen	50 fifty
6 six	16 sixteen	60 sixty
7 seven	17 seventeen	70 seventy
8 eight	18 eighteen	80 eighty
9 nine	19 nineteen	90 ninety
10 ten	20 twenty	100 a/one hundred

101 a hundred and one	200 two hundred
102 a hundred and two	301 three hundred and one
160 a hundred and sixty	484 four hundred and eighty-four
1000 a/one thousand	3,856 three thousand eight hundred and fifty-six

1st first	11th eleventh	21st twenty-first
2nd second	12th twelfth	22nd twenty-second
3rd third	13th thirteenth	30th thirtieth
4th fourth	14th fourteenth	40th fortieth
5th fifth	15th fifteenth	50th fiftieth
6th sixth	16th sixteenth	60th sixtieth
7th seventh	17th seventeenth	70th seventieth
8th eighth	18th eighteenth	80th eightieth
9th ninth	19th nineteenth	90th ninetieth
10th tenth	20th twentieth	100th hundredth

List of verbs with past tense forms

Brackets indicate that the form is not used in the text. Irregular present forms are also given.

VERB	REGULAR	IRREGULAR	VERB	REGULAR	IRREGULAR
announce	(announced)		be – am, are, is		was, were
answer	answered		believe	(believed)	
arrest	arrested		boil	(boiled)	
arrive	(arrived)		break		broke
ask	asked		bring		(brought)

VERB	REGULAR	IRREGULAR	VERB	REGULAR	IRREGULAR
burn	(burnt, burned)		miss	(missed)	
buy		bought	move	(moved)	
call	(called)		open	(opened)	
can – can		(could)	own	(owned)	
carry – carries	(carried)		pay		(paid)
climb	climbed		phone	phoned	
come		came	play	(played)	
cook	(cooked)		practise	(practised)	
cross	(crossed)		press	(pressed)	
dance	(danced)		put		(put)
dial	(dialled)		rain	(rained)	
dictate	(dictated)		read		read
die	(died)		record	(recorded)	
do – does		did	remember	remembered	
drink		drank	ring		(rang)
drive		drove	run		ran
earn	earned		say		(said)
eat		ate	see		saw
find		found	shave	shaved	
finish	finished		shine		(shone)
fly – flies		flew	shout	(shouted)	
follow	followed		show	(showed)	
free	freed		shut		(shut)
get		got	sing		(sang)
give		gave	sit		(sat)
go		went	sleep		slept
grab	grabbed		smile	(smiled)	
hang		hung	smoke	(smoked)	
happen	happened		speak		spoke
have – has		had	spell	(spelled, spelt)	
have got – has got		had	stand		(stood)
hear		heard	start	started	
help	(helped)		stay	(stayed)	
hope	(hoped)		steal		(stole)
hurry – hurries	(hurried)		stop	stopped	
interview	interviewed		study – studies	studied	
jump	jumped		swim		swam
kidnap	kidnapped		take		(took)
kill	(killed)		talk	talked	
knock	knocked		teach		(taught)
know		knew	tell		told
land	(landed)		think		thought
laugh	(laughed)		turn	turned	
learn	(learned, learnt)		type	typed	
leave		left	understand		(understood)
lift	lifted		use	used	
like	liked		wait	waited	
listen	listened		wake		woke
live	lived		walk	walked	
look	(looked)		want	wanted	
manage	(managed)		wash	washed	
mean		(meant)	watch	watched	
meet		met	wear		(wore)
mind	(minded)		work	worked	
			write		(wrote)

Pronunciations are given in the form of the International Phonetic Alphabet as used in the *Longman Dictionary of Contemporary English*. The numbers after each word indicate the unit and page number where the word first appears. G = Goodbye (final unit).

n = noun; *prep* = preposition; *conj* = conjunction; *adj* = adjective; *pron* = pronoun; *adv* = adverb; *v* = verb; *aux* = auxiliary verb; *lex v* = lexical verb; R = receptive

A

a /ə; *strong* eɪ/ 1:2
ABC /eɪ biː 'siː/ *n* 12:62
about /ə'baʊt/ *prep* 4:14
  what about? 4:13
above /ə'bʌv/ 16:85
across /ə'krɒs/ *prep* 10:49
actor /'æktəʳ/ 12:62
actress /'æktrəs/ 12:62
address /ə'dres/ *n* 6:27
advertisement
  /əd'vɜːtəsmənt/ 14:73
after /'ɑːftəʳ/ *prep* 12:64
  conj 15:78
afternoon /ˌɑːftə'nuːn/ 16:87
again /ə'gen/ 5:17
agency: travel agency 7:29
ahead /ə'hed/ 15:82
air /eəʳ/ *adj* 7:29
airline /'eəlaɪn/ G:101
airmail /'eəmeɪl/ 6:28
airport /'eəpɔːt/ 2:5
air terminal /'eə ˌtɜːmənəl/ 18:99
alarm clock /ə'lɑːm klɒk/ 6:26
all /ɔːl/ *pron* 7:30
  all right /ˌɔːl' raɪt/ 6:23
  not at all 9:42
  first of all 12:63
almost /'ɔːlməʊst/ 16:83
always /'ɔːlwəz, -weɪz/ 9:41
am /m, əm; *strong* æm/ *v* 1:4
America /ə'merəkə/ 1:2
American /ə'merəkən/ *n* 8:37
an /ən; *strong* æn/ 5:17
and /ənd, ən; *strong* ænd/ 1:1
animal /'ænəməl/ 11:55
announce /ə'naʊns/ *v* 4:15
another /ə'nʌðəʳ/ *adj* 15:80
answer /'ɑːnsəʳ/ *v* 1:2
  n 6:26
any /'eni/ *adj* 7:30
  any more /ˌeni 'mɔːʳ/ 16:86
anything /'eniθɪŋ/ 11:56
are /əʳ; *strong* ɑːʳ/ *v* 1:4
arm /ɑːm/ *n* 16:86
around /ə'raʊnd/ 16:86
arrest /ə'rest/ *v* G:105
arrival /ə'raɪvəl/ 4:15
arrive /ə'raɪv/ *v* 2:5
article /'ɑːtɪkəl/ 10:47

as /əz; *strong* æz/ *conj* 15:79
ask /ɑːsk/ *v* 1:2
at /ət; *strong* æt/ 2:5
Australia /ɒ'streɪlɪə/ 13:67
away /ə'weɪ/
  run away *v* G:105
  take away *v* 10:50

B

back /bæk/
  come back *v* 15:79
  drive back *v* 15:79
  go back *v* 13:67
bacon /'beɪkən/ 6:26
bag /bæg/ 2:6
bank /bæŋk/ *n* 9:41
bathroom /'bɑːθrʊm/ 6:23
be /bɪ; *strong* biː/ *v present* 1:1
  past 13:65
  command 18:98
  be born 13:69
  be called 5:21
beans /biːnz/ 11:55
because /bɪ'kɒz/ 13:65
bed /bed/ 6:23
bedroom /'bedrʊm/ 7:33
bedsitter /'bed'sɪtəʳ/ 7:33
beef /biːf/ 3:12
beer /bɪəʳ/ 3:12
before /bɪ'fɔːʳ/ *prep* 12:64
  conj 14:71
  adv 15:82
behind /bɪ'haɪnd/ *prep* 8:35
believe /bə'liːv/ *v* G:101
bell: "The Bell" /ðə 'bel/ 9:43
between /bɪ'twiːn/ *prep* 5:21
big /bɪg/ 3:9
Big Ben /ˌbɪg 'ben/ 1:2
bill /bɪl/ *n* 11:56
biscuit /'bɪskət/ 11:58
black /blæk/ *adj* 18:98
blindfold /'blaɪndfəʊld/ *n* 16:86
block of flats /blɒk əv 'flæts/ 8:35
blood /blʌd/ 12:61
blouse /blaʊz/ 5:18
board /bɔːd/ *v* G:101
boil /bɔɪl/ *v* 11:57
boiled /bɔɪld/ *adj* 11:55
book /bʊk/ *n* 2:6
bookcase /'bʊk-keɪs/ 9:44
booth /buːð/ 18:97
born /bɔːn/: **be born** *v* 13:69

boss /bɒs/ 8:38
Boston /'bɒstn/ 1:3
bottle /'bɒtl/ 5:18
box /bɒks/ *n* 5:18
boy /bɔɪ/ 9:37
boyfriend /'bɔɪfrend/ 11:57
bread /bred/ 7:29
break into /breɪk 'ɪntuː/ *v* G:105
breakfast /'brekfəst/ 6:26
bridge /brɪdʒ/ 12:61
briefcase /'briːfkeɪs/ 2:6
bring /brɪŋ/ *v* 5:19
Bristol /'brɪstl/ 1:3
Broadway /'brɔːdweɪ/ 1:2
brochure /'brəʊʃəʳ/ 12:63
Buckingham Palace /ˌbʌkɪŋəm 'pæləs/ 18:99
buffet car /'bʊfeɪ kɑːʳ/ 3:11
building /'bɪldɪŋ/ 16:86
burglar /'bɜːgləʳ/ 10:47
burn /bɜːn/ *v* 12:61
bus /bʌs/ 6:27
but /bʌt/ 8:38
butter /'bʌtəʳ/ 11:55
button /'bʌtn/ 18:97
buy /baɪ/ *v* 3:9
bye (= goodbye) 8:39

C

cafe /'kæfeɪ/ 11:53
calendar /'kæləndəʳ/ 13:65
calf /kɑːf/ 11:55
call /kɔːl/ *v* 2:7
  phone call /'fəʊn kɔːl/ *n* 16:88
called /kɔːld/ *adj* 5:21
"Camden Times" /ˌkæmdn 'taɪmz/ 8:38
Camden Town /ˌkæmdn 'taʊn/ 7:29
camera /'kæmərə/ 2:6
can /kən; *strong* kæn/ *aux* 4:13
can't /kɑːnt/ *aux* 6:27
canal /kə'næl/ 16:86
canteen /kæn'tiːn/ 9:43
car /kɑːʳ/ 5:17
  buffet car 3:11
car park /'kɑːʳ pɑːk/ 5:17
carrot /'kærət/ 11:55
carry /'kæri/ *v* 5:17
cassette /kə'set/ 18:97
cassette recorder /kə'set rɪ'kɔːdəʳ/ 18:97
cell /sel/ G:101

centre /'sentəʳ/ 7:30
chair /tʃeəʳ/ 6:23
cheap /tʃiːp/ 5:22
cheese /tʃiːz/ 3:12
Chicago /ʃɪ'kɑːgəʊ/ 1:3
chicken /'tʃɪkən/ 3:12
chips /tʃɪps/ 11:58
chocolate /'tʃɒklət/ 11:58
Christian /'krɪstʃən/ *adj* 10:50
cigar /sɪ'gɑːʳ/ 4:13
cigarette /ˌsɪgə'ret/ 3:11
cinema /'sɪnəmə/ 7:29
city /'sɪti/ 1:2
class /klɑːs/ 7:30
Classic /'klæsɪk/ 12:62
classroom /'klɑːs-rʊm/ 6:24
clerk /klɑːk/ 2:7
climb /klaɪm/ *v* 15:82
  climb out of *v* G:105
clock /klɒk/ 1:2
  alarm clock /ə'lɑːm klɒk/ 6:26
  o'clock /ə'klɒk/ 1:1
clothes /kləʊðz/ 5:22
cloud /klaʊd/ 17:89
coat /kəʊt/ 2:6
Coca-Cola /ˌkəʊkə 'kəʊlə/ 3:12
coffee /'kɒfi/ 3:11
cold /kəʊld/ *adj* 11:53
come /kʌm/ *v* 2:5
  come back *v* 15:79
  come on *v* 5:19
  come out of *v* 14:75
comedy /'kɒmədi/ 12:61
concert /'kɒnsət/ 15:79
contact /'kɒntækt/: **in radio contact** G:105
conversation /ˌkɒnvəseɪʃən/ 5:19
cook /kʊk/ *v* 7:31
cooker /'kʊkəʳ/ 7:33
cornflakes /'kɔːnfleɪks/ 6:26
country /'kʌntri/ 1:3
couple /'kʌpəl/ *n* 12:63
course: of course /ˌəv'kɔːs/ 6:23
cow /kaʊ/ 11:55
cowboy /'kaʊbɔɪ/ 7:29
cream /kriːm/ 11:58
  ice cream 11:56
cross /krɒs/ *v* G:103
cup /kʌp/ 11:53
curry /'kʌri/ 15:80
customs officer /'kʌstəmz 'ɒfəsəʳ/ 5:21

D

Dad /dæd/ 6:28
Dallas /ˈdæləs/ 1:3
dance /dɑːns/ v 7:31
    n 9:41
date /deɪt/ n 13:65
daughter /ˈdɔːtər/ 16:88
day /deɪ/ 8:39
dead /ded/ 8:39
dear /dɪər/ 6:28
definitely /ˈdefənətli/ 17:93
departure /dɪˈpɑːtʃər/
    G:101
dessert /dɪˈzɜːt/ 11:58
destination /ˌdestɪˈneɪʃən/
    3:10
detective /dɪˈtektɪv/ 18:95
Detroit /dɪˈtrɔɪt/ 12:64
dial /daɪəl/ v 18:97
dialogue /ˈdaɪəlɒg/ 2:6
diary /ˈdaɪəri/ 15:79
dictate /dɪkˈteɪt/ v 10:47
did /dɪd/ aux 14:72
die /daɪ/ v G:107
different /ˈdɪfərənt/ 12:61
dinner /ˈdɪnər/ 9:43
disaster /dɪˈzɑːstər/ 12:61
disc jockey /ˈdɪsk ˌdʒɒki/
    8:35
do/does /duː, dəz; strong
    dʌz/lex v 7:31
    aux 8:37
dollar /ˈdɒlər/ 16:88
door /dɔːr/ 6:23
double /ˈdʌbəl/ adj 6:23
down /daʊn/ prep 18:99
    down there 4:13
    sit down v 15:77
dress /dres/ n 5:18
drink /drɪŋk/ v 7:29, n 12:59
drive /draɪv/ v 7:31
    drive back v 15:79
driver /ˈdraɪvər/ 2:5

E

early /ˈɜːli/ 16:87
earn /ɜːn/ v 10:51
easy /ˈiːzi/ 18:97
eat /iːt/ v 11:53
egg /eg/ 3:12
either /ˈaɪðər/ adv 11:55
else:what else? /wɒt els/
    12:62
engineer /ˌendʒɪˈnɪər/ 8:38
engineering /ˌendʒɪˈnɪərɪŋ/ n
    11:57
England /ˈɪŋglənd/ 1:2
English /ˈɪŋglɪʃ/ n 7:30
    English Centre 7:30
Euston /ˈjuːstən/ 4:15
evening /ˈiːvnɪŋ/ 4:13
    good evening 6:23

every /ˈevri/ 9:41
everybody /ˈevribɒdi/ 8:35
exactly /ɪgˈzæktli/ 6:26
examination
    /ɪgˌzæmɪˈneɪʃən/ 18:95
example /ɪgˈzɑːmpəl/ 16:84
excuse me /ɪkˈskjuːz mi/
    3:11
expensive /ɪkˈspensɪv/ 5:22

F

face /feɪs/ G:104
factory /ˈfæktəri/ 8:38
fare /feər/ 3:10
father /ˈfɑːðər/ 6:27
fillet of sole /ˈfɪlɪt əv səʊl/
    11:58
film /fɪlm/ n 7:29
find /faɪnd/ v 10:50
    find out v G:102
fine /faɪn/ adj 8:39
finish /ˈfɪnɪʃ/ v 9:41
finished /ˈfɪnɪʃt/ adj 11:56
fire:gas fire 7:33
first /fɜːst/ adj 8:35; adv
    17:89
    first of all 12:63
fish /fɪʃ/ 11:55
flat /flæt/ 7:33
flight /flaɪt/ 4:15
floor /flɔːr/ 6:25
fly /flaɪ/ v 7:30
follow /ˈfɒləʊ/ v 13:65
food /fuːd/ 7:29
for /fər; strong fɔːr/ 5:17
    for now 10:50
foreign /ˈfɒrɪn/ 7:30
free /friː/ adj 13:65
    v G:105
French /frentʃ/ n 7:32
fridge /frɪdʒ/ 7:33
fried /fraɪd/ adj 11:55
friend /frend/ 5:17
from /frəm; strong frɒm/
    1:3
front /frʌnt/
    in front of 16:83
fruit /fruːt/ 7:29
    fruit salad 11:58

G

garage /ˈgærɑːʒ, -ɪdʒ/ 5:21
Gardens:Albert Gardens
    /ælbɜːt ˈgɑːdnz/ 7:34
gas fire /ˈgæs faɪər/ 7:33
gate /geɪt/ G:101
German /ˈdʒɜːmən/ n 7:32
get /get/ v 7:29
    get (home) v 9:43
    get in v 2:7
    get into v 16:86
    get off (bus) v 15:81
    get on (bus) v 15:81

get up v 6:26
girlfriend /ˈgɜːlfrend/ 11:58
give /gɪv/ 10:50
glass /glɑːs/ 11:56
go /gəʊ/ v 2:5
    go ahead v 15:82
    go back v 13:67
    go in 16:83
    go on v 15:78
    go out v 15:77
God /gɒd/
    Thank God 1:57
    My God! 18:95
going to (+ v) R16:88;
    17:89
golf /gɒlf/ 16:87
good /gʊd/ 5:19
    good evening 6:23
    good morning 2:5
goodbye /gʊdˈbaɪ/ 4:13
got /gɒt/: **have got** v 5:17
grab /græb/ v G:104
grapefruit /ˈgreɪpfruːt/
    11:54
Green Park /griːn pɑːk/
    18:99
guitar /gɪˈtɑːr/ 9:44
gun /gʌn/ 16:86

H

had /d, əd, həd; strong hæd/
    14:73
hand /hænd/ n 11:53
handbag /ˈhændbæg/ 15:79
hang up /hæŋ ʌp/ v 17:93
happen /ˈhæpən/ v 16:86
happy /ˈhæpi/ 11:57
has/have /s, z, əz, həz; strong
    hæz/ /v, əv, həv; strong
    hæv/ lex v R8:40; 11:53
has/have got v 5:17
has/have to aux 18:95
hat /hæt/ 5:17
he /i, hi; strong hiː/ 1:3
hear /hɪər/ v 4:15
hello /həˈləʊ/ 1:1
helmet /ˈhelmɪt/ 19:104
help /help/ 13:67
her /ər, hər; hɜːr/ adj 3:9
    pron 5:17
here /hɪər/ 2:5
    over here 5:19
hi /haɪ/ 5:19
High Street /ˈhaɪ striːt/ 7:29
him /ɪm; strong hɪm/ 4:13
himself /ɪmself; strong hɪm-/
    15:80
his /ɪz; strong hɪz/ adj 2:7
history /ˈhɪstəri/ 14:75
home /həʊm/ 9:43
hope /həʊp/ v 17:92
horror /ˈhɒrər/ 12:61
horse /hɔːs/ 6:27
hotel /həʊˈtel/ 2:7

hour /aʊər/ 14:73
house /haʊs/ 6:21
how /haʊ/
    how are you? 8:39
    how do you do? 8:39
    how long? 6:25
    how many? 5:22
    how much? 3:9
hungry /ˈhʌŋgri/ 11:53
hurry /ˈhʌri/ v 10:49
husband /ˈhʌzbənd/ 8:35
Hyde Park /haɪd pɑːk/ 5:21

I

I /aɪ/ 1:4
ice cream /ˌaɪs ˈkriːm/ 11:56
idea /aɪˈdɪə/ 12:62
if /ɪf/ 14:75
immediately /ɪˈmiːdɪətli/
    G:101
in /ɪn/ 1:2
Indian /ɪndɪən/ adj 15:80
information /ˌɪnfəˈmeɪʃən/
    7:29
intelligent /ɪnˈtelɪdʒənt/
    7:30
interested /ˈɪntrəstɪd/ adj
    15:82
interesting /ˈɪntrəstɪŋ/ 14:73
interview /ˈɪntəvjuː/ n 14:75
    v 15:78
into /ˈɪntə; before consonants
    ˈɪntʊ; strong ˈɪntuː/ 16:86
irregular /ɪˈregjʊlər/ 14:74
is /s, z, əz; strong ɪz/ v 1:1
    is (coming) aux 2:5
it /ɪt/ 1:1
Italian /ɪˈtælɪən/ n 7:32
    adj 11:53

J

jacket /ˈdʒækɪt/ 15:80
jeans /dʒiːnz/ 5:18
job /dʒɒb/ 7:29
jockey:disc jockey /ˈdɪsk
    ˌdʒɒki/ 8:35
joke /dʒəʊk/ n 16:88
jump /dʒʌmp/ v G:105

K

kerb /kɜːb/ G:103
key /kiː/ 6:25
kid /kɪd/ 15:82
kidnap /ˈkɪdnæp/ v 16:86
kidnapping /ˈkɪdnæpɪŋ/ 16:83
kill /kɪl/ v 17:89
kilo /ˈkiːləʊ/ 2:7
kind /kaɪnd/ n 11:53
kitchen /ˈkɪtʃən/ 7:33
knock /nɒk/ v 16:85
know /nəʊ/ (+ n) v 8:37
    (+ clause) 9:43

L

lamb /læm/ 11:55
language /'læŋgwɪdʒ/ 7:30
last /lɑːst/ *adj* 10:50
late /leɪt/ *adj* 11:57
later /'leɪtəʳ/ *adv* 12:61
laugh /lɑːf/ *v* 12:61
learn /lɜːn/ *v* 7:30
leave /liːv/ *v* 3:11
Leeds /liːdz/ 1:3
left /left/: **on the left** 4:15
leg /leg/ 16:86
less /les/ *pron* 12:63
lesson /'lesən/ 10:47
let's /lets/ (+ *v*) R11:53; 12:59
letter /'letəʳ/ 6:26
licence number /'laɪsəns ˈnʌmbəʳ/ G:104
lift /lɪft/ *n* 6:25
   v 7:30
light /laɪt/ *n* 6:26
like /laɪk/ *prep* 7:29
like /laɪk/ *v* 11:53
   I'd like 11:56
listen /'lɪsən/ *v* 1:4
   listen to *v* 2:7
live /lɪv/ *v* 8:35
Liverpool /'lɪvəpuːl/ 1:3
living room /'lɪvɪŋ ruːm/ 7:33
London /'lʌndn/ 1:2
long /lɒŋ/: **how long?** 6:25
look /lʊk/ *v* 1:1
   look at *v* 1:3
   look for *v* 7:33
Los Angeles /lɒs ˈændʒəliːz/ 12:63
lot /lɒt/: **a lot of** 10:51
loudspeaker /ˌlaʊd'spiːkəʳ/ 4:15
love /lʌv/ *n* 6:28
lunch /lʌntʃ/ 8:40

M

machine /mə'ʃiːn/ 15:79
madam /'mædəm/ 3:11
magazine /ˌmægə'ziːn/ 15:78
man /mæn/ 2:7
manage /'mænɪdʒ/ *v* 14:71
manager /'mænɪdʒəʳ/ 7:32
Manchester /'mæntʃəstəʳ/ 1:3
many /'meni/: **how many?** 5:22
map /mæp/ 7:29
Marble Arch /mɑːbəl ˈɑːtʃ/ 18:99
marmalade /'mɑːməleɪd/ 11:54
married /'mærɪd/ *adj* 8:35
maths /mæθs/ 14:75
matter /'mætəʳ/: **what's the**

matter 16:83
me /mi; *strong* miː/ 2:7
mean /miːn/ *v* 7:32
meat /miːt/ 7:29
meet /miːt/ *v* 9:45
menu /'menjuː/ 3:12
midnight /'mɪdnaɪt/ 6:26
million /'mɪljən/ 16:88
mind /maɪnd/ *v* 14:75
minute /'mɪnət/ *n* 4:14
Miss /mɪs/ 6:23
miss /mɪs/ *v* 18:99
moment /'məʊmənt/ 5:22
money /'mʌni/ 11:53
month /mʌnθ/ 7:32
more /mɔːʳ/ *adj* 10:51,
   pron R10:51; 12:63
   any more 16:86
   no more 10:50
morning /'mɔːnɪŋ/: **good morning** 2:5
mother /'mʌðəʳ/ 6:27
motorbike /'məʊtəbaɪk/ G:104
move /muːv/ *v* 16:86
Mr /'mɪstəʳ/ 2:7
Mrs /'mɪsɪz/ 7:34
much /mʌtʃ/
   how much? 3:9
   very much *adv* 11:53
music /'mjuːzɪk/ 8:35
my /maɪ/ 1:1

N

name /neɪm/ 1:1
near /nɪəʳ/ *prep* 3:11
neighbour /'neɪbəʳ/ 15:80
never /'nevəʳ/ 9:44
new /njuː/ *adj* 8:39
New York /njuː 'jɔːk/ 1:2
news /njuːz/ *n* 11:57
newspaper /'njuːsˌpeɪpəʳ/ 2:6
next /nekst/ *adj* 7:32
next to *prep* 6:23
nice /naɪs/ *adj* 8:40
   nice to meet you 9:43
night /naɪt/ 5:21
   nightclub /'naɪtklʌb/ 10:51
no /nəʊ/ 1:2; *adj* 4:13
   no more *adj* 10:50
noon /nuːn/ 10:47
not /nɒt/ 1:2
   not at all 9:42
now /naʊ/ 2:1
   for now 10:50
number /'nʌmbəʳ/ 6:24

O

o'clock /ə'klɒk/ 1:1
Odeon /'əʊdɪən/ 12:62

of /əv, ə; *strong* ɒv/ 5:18
of course /əv 'kɔːs/ 6:23
off /ɒf/ (≠ **on**) 18:97
   get off *v* 15:81
   take off *v* 17:89
office /'ɒfɪs/ 8:38
   post office 6:28
officer /'ɒfɪsəʳ/
   customs officer 5:22
often /'ɒfən/ 9:43
oh /əʊ/ 1:4
OK /əʊ'keɪ/ 2:7
old /əʊld/ 14:71
on /ɒn/ *prep* 2:5
   adv 7:29
   (≠ **off**) 18:97
   get on *v* 15:81
   go on *v* 15:78
one /wʌn/ *adj* 4:15
   this one *pron* 5:22
only /'əʊnli/ 5:22
open /'əʊpən/ *adj* 2:6
   v 5:22
or /ɔːʳ/ 3:9
order /'ɔːdəʳ/ *n* 11:56
other /'ʌðəʳ/ *adj* 4:15
   pron 5:21
our /aʊəʳ/ 8:35
out /aʊt/ *adv* 13:67
   find out *v* G:102
   go out *v* 15:77
outside /aʊt'saɪd/ *prep* 13:65
over /'əʊvəʳ/ *prep* 4:13
   over here 5:9
own /əʊn/ *v* 10:51
Oxford Circus /ˌɒksfəd 'sɜːkəs/ 15:81

P

p (pence) /piː/ 3:11
page /peɪdʒ/ 15:79
pair /peəʳ/ 5:18
Pan Am /pæn æm/ 4:15
paper (= **newspaper**) /'peɪpəʳ/ 12:62
pardon /'pɑːdn/ 1:4
parents /'peərənts/ 10:50
park /pɑːk/ 5:21
   Park Lane 5:21
   car park 5:17
   Green Park 18:99
   Hyde Park 5:21
   Regent's Park 7:29
part /pɑːt/ 7:29
passenger /'pæsɪndʒəʳ/ 5:17
passport /'pɑːspɔːt/ 5:19
past /pɑːst/ *adj* 14:74
   prep 18:99
pay /peɪ/ *v* 6:23
   pay for *v* 11:53
   pay *n* 14:73
peas /piːz/ 11:55
pence /pens/ 3:11
people /'piːpəl/ 5:20

perfume /'pɜːfjuːm/ 5:18
perhaps /pə'hæps/ 12:63
person /'pɜːsən/ 18:97
phone /fəʊn/ *v* 4:16
   n 6:26
   phone call *n* 16:88
   phone booth *n* 18:97
photograph /'fəʊtəgrɑːf/ *n* 10:51
Piccadilly /ˌpɪkə'dɪli/ 18:99
picture /'pɪktʃəʳ/ *n* 1:2
pizza /'piːtsə/ 11:53
place /pleɪs/ *n* 17:92
plane /pleɪn/ 2:5
platform /'plætfɔːm/ 3:9
play /pleɪ/ *v* 7:31
"play" button /'pleɪ ˌbʌtn/ 18:97
please /pliːz/ 1:4
pm /ˌpiː'em/ 16:87
pocket /'pɒkɪt/ 15:80
police /pə'liːs/ 10:49
policeman /pə'liːsmən/ 6:27
policewoman /pə'liːsˌwʊmən/ 5:17
porter /'pɔːtəʳ/ 2:7
postbox /'pəʊstbɒks/ 8:37
postcard /'pəʊstkɑːd/ 8:37
postman /'pəʊstmən/ 8:37
post office /'pəʊst ˌɒfɪs/ 6:28
potatoes /pə'teɪtəʊz/ 11:55
pound /paʊnd/ 3:9
practise /'præktɪs/ *v* 10:47
present /'prezənt/ *adj* 14:74
president /'prezɪdənt/ 9:41
press /pres/ *v* 18:97
price /praɪs/ 6:23
prison /'prɪzən/ 11:53
probably /'prɒbəbli/ 17:92
problem /'prɒbləm/ 17:93
programme /'prəʊgræm/ 8:35
pub /pʌb/ 5:21
put /pʊt/ *v* 2:7

Q

question /'kwestʃən/ 2:6

R

radio /'reɪdɪəʊ/ 8:35
   in radio contact G:105
rail /reɪl/ 7:29
rain /reɪn/ *v* 4:13
raw /rɔː/ 11:55
read /riːd/ *v* 6:26
really /'rɪəli/ 7:32
receiver /rɪ'siːvəʳ/ 18:97
record /'rekɔːd/ *n* 8:35
   /rɪ'kɔːd/ *v* 18:98
recorder /rɪ'kɔːdəʳ/ 18:97
recording /rɪ'kɔːdɪŋ/ 18:98
red /red/ 11:56

Regent's Park /ˈriːdʒənts paːk/ 7:29
regular /ˈreɡjʊlər/ 14:74
remember /rɪˈmembər/ v 9:42
rent /rent/ n 7:34
reporter /rɪˈpɔːtər/ 8:38
requested /rɪˈkwestəd/ G:101
reserved /rɪˈzɜːvd/ adj 6:23
restaurant /ˈrestərɔ̃/ 9:43
return /rɪˈtɜːn/ adj 3:9
rice /raɪs/ 11:55
rich /rɪtʃ/ 9:41
right! /raɪt/ 2:7
  on the right 4:15
  all right 6:23
  (≠ **wrong**) 5:18
ring /rɪŋ/ v 6:26
road /rəʊd/ 9:43
roast /rəʊst/ adj 11:55
room /ruːm/ 5:21
rope /rəʊp/ 16:86
rump steak /rʌmp steɪk/ 11:58
run /rʌn/ v 8:35
  run away v G:105

S

salad /ˈsæləd/ 11:53
  fruit salad 11:58
salami /səˈlɑːmi/ 11:53
same /seɪm/ 8:35
sandwich /ˈsænwɪtʃ/ 3:12
San Francisco /ˌsæn frənˈsɪskəʊ/ 1:3
say /seɪ/ v 1:4
scale /skeɪl/ 2:7
school /skuːl/ 7:30
science fiction /ˌsaɪəns ˈfɪkʃən/ 12:61
seat /siːt/ n 3:11
second /ˈsekənd/ adj 8:37
secretary /ˈsekrətəri/ 8:38
see /siː/ v 4:13
set /set/ : **television set** 9:44
shave /ʃeɪv/ v 15:77
she /ʃi/; strong ʃiː/ 1:3
sheriff /ˈʃerəf/ 12:61
shine /ʃaɪn/ v 6:27
shirt /ʃɜːt/ 5:18
shoe /ʃuː/ 5:22
shop /ʃɒp/ n 7:29
shout /ʃaʊt/ v 16:86
shower /ʃaʊər/ n 6:23
shut /ʃʌt/ v 15:82
  shut up /ʃʌt ʌp/ 18:98
side saɪd/ G:105
sing /sɪŋ/ v 9:44
single /ˈsɪŋɡəl/ **(ticket)** adj 3:9
  (room) 6:23
  (person) 8:39
sir /sər/ 2:7

sister /ˈsɪstər/ 13:67
sit /sɪt/ v 7:33
  sit down v 15:77
ski /skiː/ v 7:31
sleep /sliːp/ v 7:33
slot /slɒt/ 18:97
small /smɔːl/ 5:21
smile /smaɪl/ v 13:65
smoke /sməʊk/ v 4:13
snow /snəʊ/ n 11:57
so /səʊ/ 5:22
  I think so 9:45
sock /sɒk/ 5:22
sole /səʊl/ 11:58
some /sʌm/ R9:43; 11:56
someone /ˈsʌmwʌn/ 15:82
something /ˈsʌmθɪŋ/ 13:70
sometimes /ˈsʌmtaɪmz/ 9:43
son /sʌn/ 8:37
soon /suːn/ G:101
sorry /ˈsɒri/ 6:28
soup /suːp/ 3:12
spaghetti /spəˈɡeti/ 15:81
Spanish /ˈspænɪʃ/ n 7:32
speak /spiːk/ v 2:7
spell /spel/ v 7:34
stairs /steəz/ 6:25
stamp /stæmp/ n 6:27
stand /stænd/ v 6:27
  stand up v 16:86
  can't stand v 11:57
star /stɑːr/ 12:61
start /stɑːt/ v 7:32
station /ˈsteɪʃən/ 3:9
stay /steɪ/ v 6:25
steak /steɪk/ 11:53
steal /stiːl/ v 10:47
stereo /ˈsteriəʊ/ 9:44
stewardess /ˌstjuːəˈdes/ 2:5
still /stɪl/ 12:59
stop /stɒp/ v 13:68
story /ˈstɔːri/ 12:61
straight ahead /streɪt əˈhed/ 18:99
strange /streɪndʒ/ 16:85
street /striːt/ 1:2
  High Street 7:29
strong /strɒŋ/ 7:30
student /ˈstjuːdənt/ 6:24
study /ˈstʌdi/ v 11:57
subject /ˈsʌbdʒɪkt/ 14:75
suit /suːt/ n 5:18
suitcase /ˈsuːtkeɪs/ 2:5
sun /sʌn/ 8:35
supermarket /ˈsuːpəˌmɑːkət/ 7:29
sure /ʃʊər/ 10:49
swim /swɪm/ v 7:31
Swindon /swɪndn/ 14:71
switch /swɪtʃ/ n 18:97

T

table /ˈteɪbəl/ 7:33
take /teɪk/ v 5:19

take away v 10:50
take off v 17:89
taken /teɪkən/ 3:11
talk /tɔːk/ v 3:11
taste /teɪst/ n 11:57
taxi /ˈtæksi/ 2:5
tea /tiː/ 3:11
teach /tiːtʃ/ v 7:30
teacher /ˈtiːtʃər/ 6:24
telephone /ˈteləfəʊn/ 6:26
television /ˈteləˌvɪʒən/ 9:43
tell /tel/ v 5:22
tennis /ˈtenəs/ 7:31
terrible /ˈterəbəl/ 11:53
Texas Cowboy /ˈteksəs ˈkaʊbɔɪ/ 7:29
Thank God! /θæŋk ɡɒd/ 11:57
  Thank you 1:1
thanks /θæŋks/ 3:11
that /ðæt/ pron 2:5
  adj 3:10
the /ðə, ði; strong ðiː/ 1:1
their /ðər; strong ðeər/ 5:17
them /ðəm; strong ðem/ 5:19
then /ðen/ 14:75
there /ðeər/ 6:25
  there is/are v 6:23
these /ðiːz/ adj 5:20
they /ðeɪ/ 3:9
thing /θɪŋ/ 5:18
think /θɪŋk/ v 9:43
this /ðɪs/ pron 1:2
  adj 3:9
third /θɜːd/ 8:35
those /ðəʊz/ pron 6:25
thousand /ˈθaʊzənd/ 10:51
through /θruː/ 10:49
ticket /ˈtɪkət/ 2:5
tied to /taɪd tʊ/ 16:86
time /taɪm/ 1:1
  on time 16:84
  what time? 3:9
  Camden Times 8:38
tired /taɪəd/ 6:26
to /tə, tʊ; strong tuː/ 2:5
toast /təʊst/ 6:26
today /təˈdeɪ/ 7:29
toilet /ˈtɔɪlət/ 6:23
tomato /təˈmɑːtəʊ/ 3:12
tomorrow /təˈmɒrəʊ/ 17:92
too /tuː/ 1:2
Toronto /təˈrɒntəʊ/ 12:64
town /taʊn/ 8:39
traffic /ˈtræfɪk/ G:104
train /treɪn/ 3:9
tramp /træmp/ 18:95
travel agency /ˈtrævəl ˌeɪdʒənsi/ 7:29
tree /triː/ 6:27
turn (left) /tɜːn/ v 18:99
  turn on v 8:35
type /taɪp/ v 7:32

U

umbrella /ʌmˈbrelə/ 5:17
under /ˈʌndər/ 8:37
understand /ˌʌndəˈstænd/ v 10:49
unhappy /ʌnˈhæpi/ 15:77
uniform /ˈjuːnəfɔːm/ G:101
University /juːnəˈvɜːsəti/ 9:42
up /ʌp/ adv 6:25
  prep 18:99
  up there 4:13
us /əs, s; strong ʌs/ 8:37
use /juːz/ v 15:79
usual /ˈjuːʒʊəl/ 14:75
  as usual 17:93
usually /ˈjuːʒʊəli/ 9:43

V

vampire /ˈvæmpaɪər/ 12:61
van /væn/ 16:86
vanilla /vəˈnɪlə/ 11:58
Vauxhall Bridge /ˈvɒksəl brɪdʒ/ 18:99
veal /viːl/ 11:55
vegetables /ˈvedʒtəbəlz/ 7:29
verb /vɜːb/ 14:74
very /ˈveri/ 6:28
Victoria Station /vɪkˌtɔːriə ˈsteɪʃən/ 18:98

W

wait for /weɪt fɔːr/ v 5:17
waiter /ˈweɪtər/ 6:26
waiting room /ˈweɪtɪŋ ruːm/ 18:98
waitress /ˈweɪtrəs/ 6:26
wake /weɪk/ 6:26
  wake up v 16:88
walk /wɔːk/ v 5:20
  n 17:90
want /wɒnt/ (+ n) v 11:53
  want to (+ v) v R11:56; 12:59
wanted /ˈwɒntəd/ adj 15:77
war /wɔːr/ 12:61
warm /wɔːm/ 17:89
was /wəz; strong wɒs/ v 13:65
wash /wɒʃ/ v 15:77
washbasin /ˈwɒʃˌbeɪsən/ 6:23
watch /wɒtʃ/ v 8:35
water /ˈwɔːtər/ 11:56
Watford /ˈwɒtfəd/ 3:11
we /wi; strong wiː/ 4:13
wear /weər/ v 5:17
week /wiːk/ 7:34
well /wel/ 4:13
  adv 7:31
were /wər; strong wɜːr/ v 13:65

130

western /'westən/ 7:29
Westport /'westpɔːt/ 6:27
what? /wɒt/ 1:1
    conj 11:55
    what a (+*n*!) 15:78
    what about? 4:13
    what else? 12:62
    what kind? 11:53
    what time? 3:9
when? /wen/ 9:43
    conj 13:69
where? /weəʳ/ 1:3

where to? 2:5
which /wɪtʃ/ 3:9
whisky /'wɪski/ 5:18
white /waɪt/ 11:56
who? /huː/ 4:16
why? /waɪ/ 13:66
    conj 13:65
wife /waɪf/ 10:47
window /'wɪndəʊ/ 6:23
wine /waɪn/ 11:56
with /wɪð/ 6:23
woman /'wʊmən/ 3:9

wonderful /'wʌndəfəl/
    11:57
Wonderman /'wʌndəmæn/
    7:30
Wonderwoman
    /'wʌndə,wʊmən/ 7:30
word /wɜːd/ 7:32
work /wɜːk/ *v* 8:38
worried /'wʌrid/ *adj*
    16:83
write /raɪt/ *v* 1:4
wrong /rɒŋ/ 5:18

Y

year /jɪəʳ/ 10:51
yes /jes/ 1:1
yesterday /'jestədi/ 13:65
you /je, jʊ; *strong* juː/ 1:4
young /jʌŋ/ 12:63
your /jəʳ; *strong* jɔːʳ/ 1:1

Z

zoo /zuː/ 12:59